T0300413

ISLAMIC
ASSET
MANAGEMENT

Edinburgh Guides to Islamic Finance
Series Editor: Rodney Wilson

A series of short guides to key areas in Islamic finance, offering an independent academic perspective and a critical treatment.

Product Development in Islamic Banks
Habib Ahmed

Islamic Financial Services in the United Kingdom
Elaine Housby

Islamic Asset Management
Natalie Schoon

Forthcoming
Shariah Compliant Private Equity and Islamic Venture Capital
Fara Ahmad Farid

ISLAMIC ASSET MANAGEMENT

An Asset Class on its Own?

Natalie Schoon

Edinburgh University Press

To Bob – his sister's keeper

© Natalie Schoon, 2011

Edinburgh University Press Ltd
22 George Square, Edinburgh
www.euppublishing.com

Typeset in Minion Pro by
Servis Filmsetting Ltd, Stockport, Cheshire, and
printed and bound in Great Britain by
CPI Group (UK) Ltd, Croydon, CR0 4YY

A CIP record for this book is available from the British Library

ISBN 978 0 7486 3995 3 (hardback)
ISBN 978 0 7486 3996 0 (paperback)

CONTENTS

ACKNOWLEDGEMENTS

Although a pretty lonely affair at times, no book is ever written in complete isolation. Any mistakes and oversights are, of course, my own and many thanks go to everyone who has provided insights, additions and comments. First of all, I would like to thank Professor Rodney Wilson for convincing me that this book was worth writing and has a place in the series. Further thanks go to Spiro Andreadakis, Jason Kabel and Sarah Al-Ghani for their practical insights, comments and additions to various sections, to Scott Dakers for his assistance with the case studies and to Jon Winsdale for his valuable insights into the workings of indices. Finally to anyone I may have forgotten and to all friends and family for their support throughout the process of writing this work.

FIGURES

BOXES

TABLES

INTRODUCTION

Islamic, or *Sharia'a*-compliant, asset management has been growing at a rate similar to that of the Islamic financial industry as a whole, with at the time of writing close to 700 funds listed in the major databases with estimated funds under management of around 70 billion US dollars. This book reviews the Islamic asset management industry in more detail, including the types of fund offered and their operational procedures. All procedures and processes as well as the fund descriptions are generic and do not represent any particular fund or asset manager.

Fund management fits naturally within *Sharia'a*-compliant finance since Islam encourages investment and an increase in wealth for all individuals regardless of whether they are rich or poor. For those individuals with lower levels of wealth, who are less likely to be able to invest directly without losing the opportunity to diversify, the ability to invest in funds typically provides an appropriate alternative investment vehicle.

The first chapter of this book contains an overview of the principles, norms and values underpinning Islamic finance. At the risk of repeating content that appears in the other books in this series, this chapter will be of benefit to those who read this book in isolation, and whose understanding of the principles might be minimal. The differences between the different schools of thought within Islam are outside the scope of this book so the generally accepted norms and values associated with (Islamic) business ethics are

1

applied. Similarly, this book explores general accepted principles, and hence there might be differences in individual jurisdictions, though none should be significant.

After the overview of the underlying principles, Chapter 2 continues with an overview of the types of product and instrument most commonly used in Islamic asset management, while Chapter 3 provides an overview of the different types of *Sharia'a*-compliant fund. Fund operations and processing are described generically in Chapters 4 and 5, followed in Chapter 6 by an extensive review of the role of the *Sharia'a* supervisory board. Chapter 7 contains a number of case studies and is followed by a summary and concluding remarks.

CHAPTER 1
CHARACTERISTICS OF ISLAMIC FINANCE

Sharia'a provides a set of ethical principles which derive from the teachings of the Islamic faith, which governs every aspect of a Muslim's life and dealings with others including commerce. The Islamic financial system works on the basis of these principles and values, many of which are universally applicable. This chapter provides an overview of the main permissions and prohibitions in Islamic finance and aims to provide the reader with a framework for understanding the principles in the remainder of the book. The intention is not to provide a full overview of the Islamic teachings but to highlight those general principles that have an impact on Islamic asset management in particular and the way funds are structured.

1.1 Principles of Islamic ethics

The principles of Islamic ethics are often not dissimilar to the norms and values associated with the strong business ethics often advocated by professional industry bodies and the generally accepted view of social responsibility. The main distinction is that the latter are not necessarily derived from the tenets of a religion. As a result some of the ethical principles do not apply in the same way. One of the overarching principles in *Sharia'a* is justice, which defines how different parties should be dealing with each other. This applies to how parties conduct their business relations, but also, perhaps more importantly, to the way people treat each other in a larger social context. *Sharia'a* does after all govern all aspects of a Muslim's life, of which business and commerce form an integral part. The justice principle contains guidance such as the prohibition of deceit, that parties should follow the principles of fairness, and justice between parties in a contract. *Sharia'a* emphasises relativity rather than objectivity in justice, and as such looks at justice in the individual situation and, although precedents may be considered, the individual circumstances are leading.

Islamic ethics are based on six main principles, that can be summarised as follows:

1. **Stewardship of humanity on earth.** Private property is permitted on the understanding that personal wealth or property should be seen as a loan to an individual from God. Ownership is not a goal in itself, but a means to provide a good life for the recipient (as owner), his direct family and society. When using an asset or wealth, the public good should always be taken into consideration first, with the personal gain taking an important, but secondary, place. The concept of stewardship encompasses elements of both the free market economy and socialism.

2. **Integrity.** Integrity is generally described as the adherence to moral and ethical principles, soundness of moral character or honesty. Integrity is valued highly in Islam and governs all acts. The Quran specifically directs that transacting parties should deal with each other fairly and honestly.

3. **Sincerity.** All acts have to be free from deceit, hypocrisy and duplicity. In other words, all dealings have to be fair and impartial, and no information should be withheld. In business this is deemed to apply to all stakeholders, including but not restricted to employees, shareholders and clients.

4. **Piety.** Piety literally means 'devout' or 'good', and in a religious context refers to reverence for God or devout fulfilment of religious obligations. It is synonymous with respect and devotion. Within the context of *Sharia'a*, it implies that the values, norms and rules of *Sharia'a* will be implemented in all circumstances.

5. **Justness in exchange.** The principle of justness in economic exchange is associated with fairness in a transaction to all parties. Any transaction should not disadvantage either of the parties involved, for instance as a result of unreasonable prices or a pro-portionate charge for capital disregarding the result of the investment instead of the use of a profit-sharing mechanism.

6. **Righteousness and perfection at work.** Individuals have to ensure that they are able to perform their duties both personally and professionally and have to strive to achieve the highest possible level within their capability.

In addition to the foregoing, *Sharia'a* contains specific stipulations regarding charitable giving and wealth creation. *Sharia'a* does not prohibit wealth creation. To the contrary, wealth creation is deemed to be positive for the economy and is promoted. Anyone with a certain level of wealth is required to give some of it away for charitable distribution. It is beyond the framework of this book to expand on this in detail. However, suffice it to say that the Islamic system places such importance on charitable giving as to impose a compulsory tax of 2.5 per cent on average wealth annually. This is known as *zakat* and further demonstrates the emphasis in *Sharia'a* on social responsibility.

1.2 The application of Islamic ethics to business transactions

Islamic ethics do not just apply to a Muslim's personal life, but equally to all other aspects including the way they conduct their business. The high-level principles outlined in section 1.1 above provide the basis for a framework of business ethics which are reflected in a set of behavioural norms and values, described in this section.

- **Honesty and fair trade.** Any trade will have to be conducted in a fair and honest way. A trader should therefore not engage in practices such as the manipulation of weights, the hiding of defects, hoarding, cheating or taking advantage of a situation.
- **Disclosure and transparency.** The seller is required to disclose all characteristics including any potential faults, the quality of the goods and any specific characteristics to the buyer in the transaction. All components of the transaction have to be completely transparent to all parties. This is in contrast to the common law concept of 'buyer beware' or *caveat emptor*, which implies that the buyer takes some responsibility in the transaction. The buyer needs to ensure that they are aware of the quality of the goods as they will be buying 'as is' or, put otherwise, subject to all defects. Where the sale is subject to this warning, the purchaser assumes the risk that the product might be either defective or unsuitable to their needs.

- **Misrepresentation.** At all times, misrepresentation is to be avoided, and no false declarations should be made regarding the goods or the trader's own standing and ownership.
- **Selling over and above the sale of another.** Once a transaction is concluded, a third party should not attempt to interfere in the transaction by offering their own goods at a better price. Bargaining is permitted but all offers have to be made before the transaction is closed.
- **Forbidden items.** Only goods and assets that are deemed to have a value in the eyes of *Sharia'a* can be traded. Any unlawful (*haram*) goods are prohibited. Transactions and investments are screened in accordance with the screening process outlined in section 3.6.
- **Hoarding.** Notwithstanding that trade is encouraged, hoarding as well as excessive love of wealth is condemned. The emphasis is on balance, reasonableness and fairness.
- **Sale of goods and assets in the open market.** Transactions should take place in the open market and all parties have to ensure that they are aware of general market conditions and pricing prior to concluding a transaction. Neither the buyer nor the seller should take advantage of the fact that the other party is unaware of market price and conditions.
- **Avoiding taking advantage of a seller's helplessness.** Taking advantage of an individual who, under pressure or false pretences, is forced to sell an item must at all times be avoided. The buyer should, rather than taking undue advantage, offer assistance to the seller with the seller's plight. Writing off debt, revising repayment structures or other ways to assist a debtor suffering hardship is encouraged.

All the above-mentioned rules are part of the ethical framework that *Sharia'a* represents. It allows for wealth creation and trade but strongly incorporates social values. As such, the rules laid down in *Sharia'a*, at least where they govern a business, can be seen as a combination of open market and socialist economy. On the one hand prices are determined based on demand and supply and the bargaining between trading parties, whilst on the other hand also striving for greater equality, and improvement for all.

1.3 Major prohibitions

Within *Sharia'a*, three major prohibitions are defined, on usury, unnecessary uncertainty and speculation.[1] Each will be described in more detail within this section. These prohibitions do not mean that there is anything against the creation of wealth, but *Sharia'a* prescribes the ways in which wealth can be created to be via trade or investment and not by making money just from the passage of time or by taking excessive risks.

1.3.1 Usury

The literal definition of *riba* is excess or usury and, since it has no specific historical definition, it is generally interpreted as the predetermined interest collected by a lender which the lender receives over and above the principal amount it has lent out. Generally speaking, any undue excess is banned within *Sharia'a*, and although a small minority of philosophers argue in favour of interest, the general opinion is that the Quranic ban on *riba* is absolute and without qualification. *Riba* comes in various guises, but two main forms are distinguished:

1. **Excess compensation from pre-determined interest** (*riba al naseeyah*). This is the most basic form and refers to the monetary compensation for an amount provided to a borrower. As such it is the equivalent of interest paid on loans, and is linked to the amount borrowed and the duration of the loan.

2. **Excess compensation without consideration** (*riba al fadl*). This form of *riba* occurs when in a sale, or exchange of goods or services, both sides to the transaction have different values or, put differently, when there is an inequality of the exchanged counter values. Any compensation should be justified based on either a specific activity or a specific risk and neither party should be compensated in excess of the value, activity and risk.

Riba does not only apply to money, but also to any of the commodities that used to have a similar function to money: gold, silver, wheat, barley, dates and salt. In addition, it applies to any commodity that is assigned a monetary function in a country.

The prohibition of *riba* in Islamic finance means that no interest can be charged or received, which is different from conventional finance, where interest is deemed to reflect growth, economic circumstances and the availability of capital. The majority of scholars conclude that *riba* is prohibited because it creates unfairness for either the lender or the borrower, or even the economy. Local interpretations and applications vary throughout the Islamic world. In Egypt, for example, interest payments are allowed for groups of the population that cannot afford to lose their capital such as orphans and widows.

Box 1.1 The unfairness of *riba*

Riba can be viewed as unfair from three different perspectives:

For the borrower
Riba or interest creates unfairness for the borrower when the enterprise makes a profit which is less than the interest payment, turning the profit into a loss. Consequently, a consistent loss may result in bankruptcy and loss of unemployment while the loan and the interest still have to be repaid.

For the lender
Riba or interest creates unfairness for the lender in high-inflation environments when the returns are likely to be below the rate of inflation. In addition, unfairness for the lender occurs when the net profit generated by the borrower is significantly higher than the return on capital provided to the lender.

For the economy
Riba or interest can result in inefficient allocation of available resources in the economy and may contribute to instability of the system. In an interest-based economy, capital is directed to the borrower with the highest credit worthiness. In an environment where profit and loss determine the allocation of capital, the potential profitability of the project is dominant and the allocation of capital could be more efficient.

The prohibition of *riba* in Islam is similar to the prohibition of usury debated by Thomas Aquinas who, following Aristotle's teachings, argued that money does not reproduce itself, and by St Bonaventure who states that 'in itself and by itself money does not bear fruit but the fruit comes from elsewhere'. These interpretations are among the most strict when it comes to the prohibition of usury or *riba*. At the other end of the spectrum there are those who argue that interest is only prohibited when it is usurious, meaning greatly in excess of what is deemed reasonable or moderate such as extortionate prices or exorbitant rent, since that is the only time it would result in unfairness.

1.3.2 *Uncertainty and gambling*

Both unnecessary uncertainty (*gharar*) and gambling (*maysir*) are deemed to be associated with excessive risk taking and are therefore prohibited by *Sharia'a*.

Gharar is generally translated as uncertainty, but different schools of thought have different views on what *gharar* includes. The lexical meaning of *gharar* is to deceive, cheat, delude, lure, entice, and overall uncertainty, and in some cases it is defined as to unknowingly expose oneself or one's property to jeopardy. Different scholars and schools of thought interpret *gharar* slightly differently, with the three main definitions being as follows:

1. *Gharar* applies exclusively to cases of doubtfulness or uncertainty as in the case of not knowing whether something will take place or not, which for instance applies to uncertainty over the asset of the sale and can be extended to uncertainty of specifications or ownership.
2. *Gharar* only applies to the unknown, but not to cases of doubtfulness. This view is adopted when the purchaser does not know what they have bought or the seller does not know what they have sold.
3. *Gharar* applies to a combination of the above which covers both the unknown and the doubtful. *Gharar* occurs where consequences of a contract are not known. This approach is favoured by most jurists.

Uncertainty regarding the asset, the price and the delivery date all cause *gharar*. In essence, *gharar* refers to acts and conditions in exchange contracts, the full implications of which are not clearly known to the parties. The prohibition of *gharar* does not relate to situations where it is not possible to reveal all details simply because it is in the nature of the asset that not all exact details are known. The prohibition on *gharar* is similar to consumer protection regula-

---

Box 1.2 *Gharar* – an example

Recently my friend Mirjam made an offer on a house that was built in the 1850s. The seller, who has owned the house for 10 years, informed her that there were no structural problems and no damp issues. On inspection, the surveyor found that half of the beams underpinning the floor and a large part of the wall were seriously decayed as a result of a major damp problem which, given the state of the beams, was estimated to have existed for at least five years. This is a case of *gharar* since it is reasonable to assume the seller must have known of this condition, and has deliberately withheld this information.

My friend Edith on the other hand has just bought a house built in the 1960s and has asked the seller for information regarding the foundation of the house. The seller told her that as far as he was aware it was a solid concrete foundation. A survey was carried out which concluded the same based on the time of build and other available information. Although there is uncertainty involved since a foundation cannot necessarily be inspected, this is deemed to be trivial *gharar* and is permissible. Some trust has to exist in this case between buyer and seller, as the seller is not deliberately withholding any information but is relaying the information as he knows it.

---

tion in Western laws which tend to include clauses relating to the requirement to enhance clarity and transparency. In addition, financial regulators are actively enforcing regulation associated with the prohibition of unclear and misleading statements in any form of advertising and any other information banks provide to their clients.

Gharar occurs in different parts of a transaction:

1. **Subject matter.** *Gharar* in the subject matter occurs when the actual goods or services involved in a transaction are not clearly defined or are unknown. For example, if I offer to sell my car for £10,000 there is *gharar* in the subject matter since the car is not specified in sufficient detail. As soon as the uncertainty is removed, for example by specifying the details of the product or service, the contract becomes valid. *Gharar* of the subject matter does not apply when the contract concerns mass-produced goods, since these are by definition specific.

2. **Price.** Equally, when the goods or services are defined in sufficient detail but the price is uncertain, the contract is subject to *gharar*. Uncertainty in price can for instance occur when the price is subject to a valuation, and can be removed by agreeing the price.

3. **Over a period of time.** Payment may be deferred as long as the terms of the payment are specified. *Gharar* occurs when the payment terms are not specified in detail, for instance when the payment date is dependent on an event in the future which is certain to happen although it is uncertain when.

4. **Ignorance.** *Gharar* occurs when one of the parties in a transaction is unaware of market practice or price.

Maysir or speculation occurs when there is a possibility of total loss to one party in the contract, and is associated with games of chance or gambling. It has elements of *gharar*, but not every *gharar* is *maysir*. Anything related to uncertainties of life and business activities involving an element of chance and risk taking are not subject to either *gharar* or *maysir*. One of the distinguishing features of Islamic finance is the sharing of risk between transacting parties such as entrepreneurs and financiers, and hence not all types of risk taking are prohibited. The following risk types are generally defined:

1. **Entrepreneurial risk incurred in the normal course of business.** Enterprises make profits and occasionally incur losses. Generally profits tend to outstrip any losses since otherwise the enterprise would be an unattractive proposition. Willingness to take an entrepreneurial risk is not deemed to be a moral evil and is encouraged by Islam in the form of investments as well as setting up a business, which typically takes the form of a partnership or *musharaka* in which all partners provide capital and expertise to the venture. It is fulfilling a need that a society cannot do without, and the risk and associated uncertainty are permissible.

2. **Possibility of natural disasters and calamities occurring.** These risks are completely out of the control of an individual or business and are acceptable risks to take. Protection against these risks, also known as *force majeure*, by means of *Sharia'a*-compliant mutual insurance is permissible.

3. **Risks that arise from uncertainties related to activities voluntarily undertaken which are not part of everyday life and arise from types of 'game' people devise.** The risks involved are unnecessary for the individual (the risk does not have to be taken) and unnecessary

for society (taking the risk does not add any economic value to the wealth of the society). These risks are akin to gambling which is prohibited. Examples are lotteries, casinos or speculative transactions.

1.4 Prohibited industries

In addition to industries and economic activities that are generally prohibited in society such as illegitimate drugs and illegal weapons trade, there are a number of other industries that are prohibited (*haram*) within the framework of *Sharia'a*. These industries are out of bounds to any investor that wishes to invest their funds in line with *Sharia'a* principles, and extends beyond the individual to all Islamic financial services including asset management, wealth management and general investments. *Sharia'a* prohibits the following industries:

- **Conventional banking and insurance.** Conventional banking and insurance is associated with interest and is therefore not permissible.
- **Alcohol.** The prohibition of alcohol for consumption extends to distilling, marketing and sale and includes working in the industry.
- **Pork-related products and non-compliant food production.** The consumption of pork and investing in related industries is expressly forbidden. In addition, non-compliant food production is also prohibited and covers everything which is not prepared in a *halal* way, among others meat which is not slaughtered in an acceptable fashion.
- **Gambling.** This covers not only casinos and betting shops, but also bingo halls, online betting and any other form of gambling.

- **Tobacco.** As with alcohol, this includes the production, marketing and sale of tobacco and associated products.
- **Adult entertainment.** Any activity associated with adult entertainment including escort services, brothels and movies with explicit sexual content.
- **Weapons, arms and defence manufacturing.**

1.5 Prohibitions and economics at a glance

Although Islamic finance works within the framework of *Sharia'a,* it is important to realise that the principles applied to business are not associated with the way people practise their beliefs, but with Islamic economics and commercial transactions. These principles are strongly based on social justice, trust and accountability, which show clearly in the principles outlined in this chapter. These ethical dimensions are not unique to Islam: they can for example be found in Adam Smith's *The Theory of Moral Sentiments* (1795) which in turn reflects views similar to, among others, Ibn Rushd, Thomas Aquinas and Aristotle.

The prohibitions on interest, short selling, excessive speculation, excessive debt, debt trading, excessive leverage and others are all resulting from the ethical framework which promotes honesty, fair trade, open markets, disclosure and transparency. In the same vein, misrepresentation, hoarding and taking undue advantage are discouraged.

1.6 *Sharia'a* and asset management

Islamic asset management, like any other part of the Islamic financial industry, needs to work within the ethical framework identified by *Sharia'a.* As a result, the fund framework, any investments, leverage and all processing needs to be compliant with the principles of *Sharia'a.* Islamic funds can for example not invest in conventional banking and insurance companies as a result of the prohibition on *riba*. Equally, they will not be able to invest in conventional bonds, put money on an interest-bearing deposit, invest in industries that are prohibited, or purchase collateralised debt obligations (CDO) or other speculative instruments.

The next chapters of this book will highlight the challenges associated with processing, how Islamic funds select their investments, the types of instrument they have available and the different structures.

Note

1. The content of this section is largely based on pages 19–23 of *Islamic Banking and Finance* (Schoon 2008).

CHAPTER 2
CONTRACTS AND STRUCTURES FOR ISLAMIC ASSET MANAGEMENT

Asset management has historically developed to provide investors with investment and diversification opportunities they would not have been able to achieve individually. This chapter will review the development of the asset management industry, including Islamic asset management solutions. It contains an overview of the current state of the Islamic asset management market, and a brief overview of geographical spread and the main types of fund currently available in the market.

2.1 The definition of a fund

The *Oxford Dictionary of Finance and Banking* (1997) provides the following definition for the term 'fund': '1. A resource managed on behalf of a client by a financial institution. 2. A separate pool of monetary and other resources used to support designated activities.' In asset management terms a fund is typically a combination of these two: a separate pool of resources managed on behalf of one or more clients.

From an investor's point of view, an investment in a fund is typically a financial investment made with the expectation of a monetary gain. The *Oxford Dictionary of Finance and Banking* defines a financial investment as:

The purchase of assets, such as securities, works of art, bank and building-society deposits, etc., with a primary view to their financial return, either as income or capital gain. This form of financial investment represents a means of saving. The level of financial investment in an economy will be related to such factors as the rate of interest, the extent to which investments are likely to prove profitable, and the general climate of business confidence.

For the purpose of this book, an investment in a fund equates to the purchase of assets (the fund units) with a view to generating monetary return, typically in the medium to long term. From the investor's perspective, there are many advantages to investing in funds rather than directly investing in companies, art or other assets. The return on investment tends to be higher than the return on a deposit account which is in part due to the longer time horizon and in part to the increased risk the investor takes. As described in Chapter 3, different types of fund cater for different risk appetites and, as a result, a different level of potential profit or loss. However, even the types of fund with the lowest risk profiles, such as enhanced cash funds, tend to provide the potential for a higher return than deposit accounts, which is mainly due to a combination of a longer time horizon and the possibility of investing in a more diversified asset.

Diversification is an important tool for an investor since it reduces volatility, spreads risks and smoothes returns. This can be achieved by actively managing a portfolio of direct investments. However, this would require the investor to spend significant amounts of time monitoring the portfolio and to have a broad knowledge base relating to the market. In addition, the investor would likely incur significant transaction costs, which have a much lesser impact on larger investment amounts. For the majority of individual investors this is not a feasible option because of monetary and/or time constraints. Investing in one or more funds offers a viable alternative. On the one hand, the required investment amounts are typically lower which makes funds accessible to a larger audience. On the other hand, the fund manager has large amounts of assets under management which allows for larger diversification opportunities and lower transaction costs, and has access to large-scale resources to analyse investment opportunities and monitor current investments. As a result, investing in funds gives the investor access to the benefits of large-scale investments against relatively small invested amounts.

2.2 The definition of a *Sharia'a*-compliant fund

Within Islam, investing in enterprises and assets is encouraged not just because of the wealth increase for the individual investor, but also because it advances the economy and at the same time allows others to increase their wealth. This in turn results in better wealth distribution.

Conventional and Islamic investors have common objectives such as capital preservation, yield maximisation and ensuring a balance between liquidity and profitability, in addition to which Islamic investors look for *Sharia'a* compliance. Not every investor has the time to manage their investments actively or the level of wealth to allow for sufficient diversification and reasonable cost. Similar to conventional investors, Islamic investors often turn to fund or asset management solutions. From an Islamic investor's perspective there is another advantage of investing in funds. The fund manager of a *Sharia'a*-compliant fund assumes full responsibility for the *Sharia'a* compliance of the investments. In the event of direct investments, initial and ongoing monitoring of *Sharia'a* compliance is the responsibility of the individual investor, is difficult to ensure and is time consuming, resulting in uncertainty as well as additional cost.

Like conventional investment managers, Islamic investment managers can invest in a wide range of Islamic and conventional products and asset classes including shares and other securities. The main difference between conventional and Islamic investment managers is that the latter will have to ensure that their individual investments, as well as the fund, remain compliant with *Sharia'a*. In addition, Islamic fund managers cannot use derivatives, pay or receive interest or apply stock lending techniques.

The Accounting and Auditing Organization for Islamic Financial Institutions (AAOIFI) defines a fund as follows:

> Funds are investment vehicles, which are financially independent of the institutions that establish them. Funds take the form of equal participating shares/units, which represent the shareholders'/unitholders' share of the assets, and entitlements to profits or losses. The funds are managed on the basis of either a mudaraba or wakala contract. (AAOIFI financial accounting standard 14, appendix B)

It is clear that besides the way in which a *Sharia'a*-compliant fund is managed, the definition of a fund does not vary significantly from the general definition of a fund as outlined previously. From an investor perspective, there is equally hardly any difference in the investor's objectives.

The same standard further specifies that:

> Investment funds are permissible by Shari'a. Because funds are a form of collective investment that continue throughout their term, the rights and duties of participants are defined and restricted by the common interest, since they relate to third par-

ties' rights. Hence, in case the fund is managed on the basis of agency the shareholders/unitholders waive their right to management, redemption or liquidation except in accordance with the limitations and conditions set out in the statutes and by-laws. (AAOIFI financial accounting standard 14, appendix B)

2.3 Islamic fund management structures

The general fund management structure is shown in Figure 2.1. The fund investors are generally known as the *rab al mal*, or the providers of capital. The relationship between the investors and the fund is based on a *mudaraba* or *wakala* contract in which the fund manager is either the *mudarib* or business manager, who provides investment knowledge, expertise and experience or, in cases where the fund management contract is based on a *wakala* contract, the *wakil* or agent. When it comes to the investment process however, the fund manager takes on the role of the capital provider on behalf of the fund unit holders.

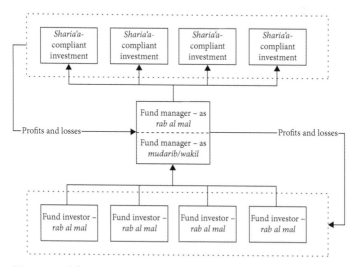

Figure 2.1 *Islamic asset management structure*

2.3.1 Mudaraba

The *mudaraba* is a passive partnership contract in which only one of the partners contributes capital (the *rab al mal*) while the other (the *mudarib*) contributes knowledge, skill and expertise. Although the investor can impose certain mutually agreed conditions in the contract, the investor has no right to interfere in the day-to-day operations of the business. Due to the fact that one of the partners is running the business and the other is solely providing capital, the relationship between the partners is founded in trust, with the investor having to rely heavily on the *mudarib*, their ability to manage the business and their honesty when it comes to profit share payments. In its simplest form, the *mudaraba* contract can be depicted as shown in Figure 2.2.

Once the contract has been agreed between the partners, the process can be broken down into the following main components:

1. **Capital injection.** The investor, also known as *rab al mal*, provides capital to the project or company. Generally an investor will not provide any capital unless a clearly defined business plan is presented to them. In

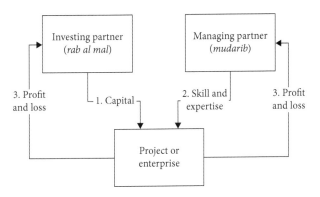

Figure 2.2 *Simple* mudaraba *structure*

this structure, the investor pays up 100 per cent of the capital.

2. **Skill and expertise.** The *mudarib* or business manager's contribution to the partnership is their skill and expertise in the chosen industry or area.

3. **Profit and loss.** If all goes well, the project will accrue profits which will be shared between the partners according to the ratios agreed in the original contract. Any losses are solely attributable to the investor due to the fact that they are the sole provider of all capital to the project. In the event of a loss, the business manager does not receive any compensation (*mudarib* share). The only exception to this is when the business manager has been negligent, in which case they become liable for the total loss.

The investor or *rab al mal* in a *mudaraba* transaction is only liable to the extent of the capital they have provided. As a result, the business manager or *mudarib* cannot commit the business for any sum which is over and above the capital provided.

The *mudaraba* contract can usually be terminated at any time by either of the parties giving a reasonable notice. Typically, conditions governing termination are included in the contract so that any damage to the business or project is eliminated in the event that the investor would like to take his equity out of the venture.

Mudaraba contracts are particularly suited to fund management since two distinct roles can be defined in the process, that of the investor and that of the fund manager, and the latter typically does not invest any money in the funds managed. The fund manager is paid a *mudarib* fee representing their efforts and can in addition be paid a share of the profits of the fund as an incentive. The balance between the *mudarib* fee and the profit share needs to be determined carefully in order to ensure that the fund manager is suitably remunerated while at the same time being appropriately incentivised to act in the best interest of the investors.

2.3.2 Wakala

A *wakala* agreement is the agreement that governs the principal–agent relationship between two parties where one party is requesting another to act on its behalf. The application of the *wakala* agreement is varied and can range from appointing an agent (*wakil*) to purchase or sell an asset, to the investment of funds. The agent or *wakil* is entitled to a fee for their services. In addition, any profit made by the agent over and above a pre-agreed anticipated profit rate could be granted to them as an incentive. Within the context of *Sharia'a*-compliant fund management, the *wakala* agreement can be used for the purpose of managing the fund, but also as a liquidity instrument within the range of products available to the fund manager. The application of the latter is reviewed in more detail in Chapter 3.

2.4 Diversification and the risk-free asset

Modern portfolio theory, first introduced by Markowitz (1952) and further developed by Sharpe (1964), argues that by choosing the optimum combination of different assets it is possible to maximise returns and minimise risk. The investor's aim is to select a collection of assets with a lower average risk than the individual assets. Risk is reduced by selecting the different investments in such a way that they are not perfectly positively correlated or, in other words, investments that do not move in the same way during the economic cycle. Bonds and shares are an example of assets that are not perfectly positively correlated. Generally speaking, higher risk equates to potentially higher returns as well as the potential for significantly higher losses. Modern portfolio theory attempts to build a portfolio in such a way that higher returns can be achieved at lower levels of risk. Although much debated, there is still a lot of truth in the basic concepts linking diversification, risk and return which allows the investor to achieve the same return at a lower level of risk.

The risk-free asset is a hypothetical asset which pays a return that is deemed to be associated with very low risk. Typically, the asset is issued by a government with an AAA rating and is generally short term, for example US Treasury bills or UK gilts. The default risk on these securities is very low, they pay a fixed return and they are uncorrelated to any other assets. The risk-free asset provides the minimum return possible.

2.4.1 Diversification and the risk-free asset in Islamic finance

Both diversification and risk-free rates are more challenging subjects for *Sharia'a*-compliant fund managers. A *Sharia'a*-compliant investor excludes certain industries that are considered to be *haram* or unlawful which results in a smaller investment universe and hence reduces the potential for diversification. Reduced diversification is generally associated with increased volatility, and hence higher risk to achieve a comparable level of returns.

There are only very few governments issuing *Sharia'a*-compliant instruments which makes replicating a risk-free asset significantly more difficult. As the industry develops, more countries have an interest in issuing part of their national debt in a *Sharia'a*-compliant format, which will alleviate this situation. However, at the time of writing, many investors and fund managers will be hampered by the limited availability of a risk-free asset.

2.5 *Sharia'a*-compliant product types

There are a variety of *Sharia'a*-compliant transaction types that can be applied to funds as well as other Islamic financial solutions. The main transaction types are briefly explained in this section.

Due to the prohibitions on interest, gambling, uncertainty and short selling, Islamic financial products are not the same as conventional financial products. Accumulation of wealth is encouraged but not by making money with money. As a result, any financial structure will be required to either have an underlying asset or an underlying enterprise. The transaction types detailed here are not intended to provide a full overview of all available transaction types in the market, only a high-level overview of those that are applicable to *Sharia'a*-compliant asset management.

2.5.1 *The asset*

Any Islamic financial transaction needs to be free of interest, gambling and uncertainty and in addition needs to be associated with either an asset or an enterprise. The asset of the transaction needs to fulfil a number of criteria:

1. The asset needs to be permissible according to *Sharia'a*, which means that it should not be involved with any of the forbidden items detailed in section 3.6.1.
2. The asset needs to exit at the time it is transacted. There are exceptions to this rule where the purpose of the transaction is associated with growing, building or producing the asset.

3. The asset needs to be owned by the seller, which implies that the seller cannot sell an asset he does not own and, consequently, cannot enter into a short-selling transaction.

4. The seller needs to be able to deliver the asset. Although absolute delivery is desirable, it is recognised that this is not necessarily possible for immovable goods or goods in transit. An example of non-absolute delivery would be if the seller has bought a consignment of ladies' shoes which are currently shipped by sea. The seller is the owner, but has no direct access to the shoes. However, the seller can draw up the documentation for the buyer to collect the goods, or instruct the transport company to deliver to the address designated by the buyer. In this case the seller's ability to deliver is non-absolute and permitted.

5. The asset needs to be specific and determined without any uncertainty. This could for example be achieved by selecting it from a shop shelf or specifying all details in a contract.

The remainder of this chapter deals with the different products available in Islamic finance that are of use to the *Sharia'a*-compliant fund investor.

2.5.2 Direct investments and venture capital

Direct investments and venture capital can be seen as partnership agreements. There are two different structures for the partnership contracts in Islamic finance, *musharaka* and *mudaraba*, with *mudaraba* being a subset of the *musharaka* contract. The main difference between the two structures is related to what the partners provide to the partnership. The *mudaraba* contract is detailed in section 2.3.1 and in addition to being used to govern the relationship between the investor and the fund manager can also be used for private equity or venture capital investments.

Musharaka means 'sharing', which in financial instrument terms translates to a partnership- or joint venture-type arrangement. Contrary to the *mudaraba* contract in which the role of the parties is divided between capital providers and business managers, in the *musharaka* contract each and every one of the partners provides a share of capital as well as skill and expertise to the joint venture. Profits are shared in accordance with the ratio that is agreed in the contract and which generally reflects the contribution of each of the parties. Losses are distributed in accordance to the proportion of capital provided. *Musharaka* contracts are particularly useful for investments in private equity, and are favoured by financial institutions due to the additional comfort that is provided by the fact that the business managers are also investing some of their own capital. In a *musharaka* transaction, the bank is typically a sleeping partner, which implies they have no say in the day-to-day operations of the enterprise. The partners in the *musharaka* contract have unlimited liability. In its simplest form, the *musharaka* contract can be depicted as in Figure 2.3.

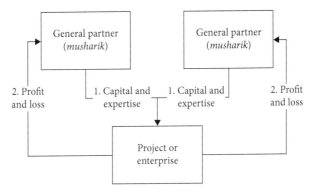

Figure 2.3 *Simple* musharaka *transaction*

Once the contract has been agreed between the partners, the process can be broken down into the following two main components:

1. **Capital and expertise.** All partners bring a share of the capital and can contribute to the management of the business or project as well. The partners do not have to provide equal amounts of capital or equal amounts of expertise.

2. **Profits and losses.** In a perfect world the project will accrue profits which will be shared between the partners according to the ratios agreed in the original contract. To the contrary, any losses that the project might incur are distributed to the partners strictly in proportion to capital contributions. Although profits can be distributed in any proportion by mutual consent, it is not permissible to fix a lump sum profit for any single partner.

Musharaka contracts are generally for a relatively longer term and can be terminated due to liquidation, sale or one of the partners buying out the other.

From the fund manager's perspective, *musharaka* contracts are particularly suitable for private equity and venture capital investments since the business manager also has a capital stake in the transaction.

Profit sharing and loss distributions and the impact on investors

A significant challenge with *musharaka* and *mudaraba* contracts is that they have the potential to be asymmetric which is directly resulting from the principles of profit sharing and loss distribution. Profits are agreed in accordance with the ratio specified in the documentation of the contract, which could be based on any metric agreed between the parties.

Recalling the principles of *Sharia'a* outlined in Chapter 1, in particular fairness, transparency, integrity and sincerity, the profit share should be fair between the parties and recognise the value of the contributions, be they capital or skills and expertise.

Not all profits are necessarily paid out to the investor: there is likely to be a significant proportion that will be reinvested. This proportion of the profits will increase the individual's share of capital, but cannot be realised until the share in the venture is sold.

Losses are, however, distributed purely in proportion to the capital provided, which potentially disadvantages the person providing the majority of or, in the case of a *murabaha* transaction, all of the capital without any recourse to the other party.

Limited and unlimited liability

The losses for the partners in a *mudaraba* transaction are limited to the capital they have provided. They are therefore not responsible for any losses over and above the invested amount.

In a *musharaka* transaction, all partners have unlimited liability for all losses, which means they can be held responsible beyond the level of their investment. The reason for the difference in liability between *mudaraba* and *musharaka* is related to the fact that in a *musharaka* contract all partners have a level of responsibility for overseeing the operations, even though it may be only at a very high level.

2.5.3 *Public and private equity*

Investing in stocks and shares is permitted as long as they are compliant with *Sharia'a*. The criteria for *Sharia'a-*

compliant stock selection are identified in AAOIFI standard 21, which includes two distinct screening criteria: an industry screen and a financial screen. The industry screen is a negative screening process that specifically excludes certain industries such as conventional banking and finance, weaponry and defence, and adult entertainment. The financial screen includes criteria regarding the acceptable level of conventional debt and recognises that in a global economy it may be difficult to identify investments that are completely *Sharia'a* compliant at all times. The consensus among *Sharia'a* scholars is that a maximum level of 5 per cent of non-*Sharia'a*-compliant activity can be allowed although any profit attributable to these activities will have to be purified by donating it to charity. The selection criteria are detailed in section 3.6.

Investing in public shares is not a partnership agreement such as the *musharaka* and *mudaraba* transactions, but rather a purchase and sale transaction between two parties. There is however some form of profit and loss sharing included in an equity investment. Dividends are a form of profit share and are proportionate to capital provided. However, not all profits are necessarily distributed since some profits are retained. In addition, equity investors are not directly responsible for losses although they can technically lose the full value of their investment. Only when the investor sells their shares do they realise the full potential of their profit or loss.

2.5.4 *Interbank liquidity*

Interbank liquidity can be provided using three main instruments: *wakala*; commodity *murabaha*; and *tawarruq*.

Wakala

Similar to the structure described in section 2.3.2, a *wakala* contract can be used to place funds with an Islamic financial institution to invest in a *Sharia'a*-compliant manner. Generally, the agent (*wakil*) provides an indicative profit and all additional profits will be retained by the agent as an incentive. The *wakala* contract can only be executed between Islamic financial institutions, since in that case there is absolute certainty that all investments will be *Sharia'a* compliant.

Commodity *murabaha* and *tawarruq*

In the event one of the parties is a conventional financial institution, *Sharia'a* compliance of either the investment or the capital is not automatically guaranteed. In order to overcome this, the parties ensure the transaction is *Sharia'a* compliant by introducing an asset which is purchased and sold as part of the transaction. One of the important characteristics of these transaction types is that as part of the contract between the buyer and the seller, all elements are known to all parties. The buyer has full knowledge of the price and quality of goods bought; they are aware of the exact amount of mark-up paid to the seller and the date on which this is required to be paid.

A commodity *murabaha* is also referred to as a deferred payment sale or instalment credit sale and uses a commodity, usually a base metal, as the underlying asset for the transaction. The intention is to replicate conventional money market transactions (the interbank market), and the banks or fund managers do not typically hold the underlying commodity or have a requirement for it. The metals are purchased and sold solely to facilitate interbank liquidity in accordance with *Sharia'a* principles.

Due to the fact that commodity *murabaha* transactions

are fixed rate, they are typically short term with a maximum term of one year. In addition to commodity *murabaha,* interbank liquidity is sometimes provided using a *tawarruq* transaction, which is equally using a base metal as the underlying commodity.

The criteria for a commodity to be considered suitable are that it should be non-perishable, freely available and can be uniquely identified. Any commodities that were originally used as a means of exchange or money – gold, silver, barley, dates, wheat and salt – are not acceptable.

The aim of the commodity *murabaha* is either to place or to take a deposit to generate a return. Figure 2.4 shows the process flow for a commodity *murabaha* used for a deposit given.

The steps for a deposit given as outlined in Figure 2.4 are defined as follows:

1. The Islamic financial institution offers the counterparty to sell warrants signifying an amount of base metal on a deferred payment basis, against a pre-agreed mark-up and to be paid on a pre-agreed date.
2. The counterparty accepts the offer from the Islamic financial institution.
3. The counterparty becomes the principal owner of the warrants.

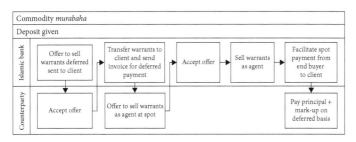

Figure 2.4 *Process flow for a deposit given*

4. The counterparty requests the Islamic financial institution to sell the warrants as its agent.
5. The Islamic financial institution sells the warrants against immediate payment to a metal broker.
6. The metal broker makes an immediate payment to the counterparty via the Islamic financial institution.

The net result of the above movements of warrants and cash is that the counterparty now holds an amount of money against an offsetting payment to the Islamic bank for a pre-agreed principal plus a mark-up at a pre-agreed future date thus creating a synthetic deposit. Each of the steps is agreed between parties before it is executed.

In a deposit taken, which is also known as a reverse commodity *murabaha*, the parties are reversed with the net result being that the Islamic financial institution holds an amount of money against an offsetting payment to the counterparty for a pre-agreed principal plus a mark-up at a pre-agreed future date thus creating a synthetic loan.

A widely used variation on the commodity *murabaha* is the *tawarruq* transaction. The process outlined above as well as the economic function of the transaction are the same, but all steps in the transaction are pre-agreed between the parties prior to the start of the contract. One of the potential problems with this is that if the transaction falls through at any point, ownership of the asset may not be clear. The majority of *Sharia'a* scholars have historically approved the transaction for reason of necessity, in other words the *tawarruq* contract is a valuable instrument enabling the industry to develop. Not only does it allow the Islamic financial institution to transact with conventional institutions in a *Sharia'a*-compliant manner, but it also ensures that there are no adverse tax implications such as value added tax (VAT) or double stamp duty. Approval is generally subject to certain conditions such as an auditable ownership transfer of the commodity and separation of the purchase and sale arrangements.

The majority of commodity *murabaha* and *tawarruq* transactions use London Metal Exchange (LME) base metals as an asset since they meet all criteria for a commodity and are easily identifiable via warrants. The purchase and sale transactions for the commodities are however over the counter and do not go via the exchange since the LME is a futures market. The warrant is a bearer document and signifies ownership of the underlying metal to the holder. Warrants are sold over the counter (OTC) and are available for a multitude of LME products, though not all are acceptable from a *Sharia'a* perspective, since the underlying asset needs to be non-perishable. Plastic, for example, does not meet this requirement. The most commonly used metals are aluminium and copper, primarily because of their large contract size and relatively higher price per warrant which ensures the number of warrants to be purchased is low. Any commodity price risk is avoided via each of the following means:

1. **Timing of purchase and sale**. All purchase and sale transactions of commodities take place on the same day.
2. **Use of premium warrants**. To mitigate the risk of any price movement during the day, the warrants that are used within these transactions are those that are trading at a premium to the market price. The reason that these warrants trade at a premium is often due to the location of the warehouse.

In comparison to conventional deposits, commodity *murabaha* and *tawarruq* transactions attract an additional cost associated with the purchase and sale of the warrants which could be dependent on volume and contract size.

For longer-dated contracts, this is not necessarily an issue as the additional cost is spread over a longer period. It does however have a significant impact on the pricing of shorter-dated deposits.

2.5.5. *Short-term placements*

A *salam* contract is a purchase contract in which full payment is made now against future delivery of an asset. The *salam* contract is exempt from two of the conditions of contract that normally apply at the time of contracting: the asset does not have to be in existence, and the seller does not need to have ownership. *Salam* contracts are typically short term (one to three months) but could be entered into for longer periods.

Due to the fact that the goods still need to be produced, they can only be transacted on the basis of their attributes such as type, quality and quantity but cannot be attributed to an individual supplier, factory, batch or field. Any good that cannot be specified by its quality and quantity (for example, precious stones) cannot be the subject of a *salam* transaction. The seller has a contractual obligation to deliver the specified quantity and quality at the agreed delivery date, even if this implies he has to purchase the specified quantity from another. In Islamic finance, this transaction type can be used for short-term production finance or agriculture.

For Islamic fund management, the contract can be applied to short-term interbank placements or to replicate a short sale. The latter is less common, but is applied for instance in Islamic hedge funds.

2.5.6 *Leasing*

Leasing or *ijara* transactions have a predictable return and are defined as a bilateral contract allowing for the transfer of the usufruct. This implies that there is one party (the lessor) who allows another party (the lessee) to use their asset against the payment of a rental fee. Two main types of leasing transactions exist: operating and finance leases. Operating leases are called *ijara* in Arabic; finance leases are named *ijara wa iqtina* (lease with transfer of ownership) or *ijara muntahia bittamleek* (lease ending in ownership) to signify that at the end of the transaction period the ownership of the asset is transferred to the lessee. A finance lease is distinguished from an operating lease by the absence or presence of a promise to purchase the asset at the end of the lease. In a finance lease, this promise to purchase or purchase undertaking is provided at the start of the contract. Under no circumstances can the lease be conditional on the purchase undertaking (that is, the lessor cannot stipulate they will only lease the asset if the lessee signs a purchase undertaking). Only assets that are tangible, non-perishable, valuable, identifiable and quantifiable are suitable for leasing transactions.

In an operational lease the lessor leases the asset to the lessee for a pre-agreed period. The lessee pays pre-agreed periodic rentals which can either be fixed for the period or floating with periodical re-fixing. The latter is usually done by linking it to a conventional index such as the London Interbank Offer Rate (LIBOR). At the end of the contract term, the contract can be extended, or the lessee can return the asset to the lessor. The lessor takes a view on the residual asset value at the end of the lease term, takes ownership risk, and runs the risk that the asset will be worth less than anticipated at the end of the lease term.

In a finance lease the lessor amortises the asset over the term of the lease and the ownership transfers to the lessee either at the end of the lease, or gradually over the duration. Similar to an operating lease, rentals can be fixed for the period or floating. As part of the lease agreement, the lessee provides the lessor with a unilateral purchase undertaking which specifies the amount at which the lessee will acquire the asset upon expiry of the lease.

Three options are possible:

1. **Gift.** In this case, the lessor has completely amortised the asset and once all rentals are paid, there is no further payment required from the lessee to obtain the asset.
2. **Against fixed payment.** At the end of the lease, the lessee becomes the owner of the asset once they have paid the purchase amount agreed in the contract.
3. **Against market value.** At the end of the lease, the lessee becomes the owner of the asset once they have paid the market value to the lessor.

In practice, options 1 and 2 are most common.

From an Islamic asset management perspective, the lease structure that is most suitable is the finance lease which is fully amortised over the life of the transaction since this provides the smoothest return profile and avoids any residual risk.

2.5.7 *Project finance*

Like a *salam* contract, an *istisna* contract is a purchase contract for future delivery of an asset, and is exempt from the same two conditions regarding the asset, ownership and existence. Unlike the *salam* contract, in an *istisna* contract, the payment to the producer or contractor of the asset does not have to be in full in advance. Payment is likely to be in various instalments in line with the progress made on the development of the asset and is therefore well suited to project finance and construction.

2.5.8 *Foreign exchange*

The exchange of money in one currency against another currency is permitted as long as the counter values are of an equal amount and are exchanged immediately. In a finance context, this means that foreign exchange spot transactions are generally acceptable. In addition, the following criteria are applicable to these transactions:

- The contract of exchange should not be subject to conditional options such as 'I will sell you £2,000 in return for €2,500 if the GBP/EUR exchange rate moves above €1.25 per British pound.'
- The foreign exchange transaction cannot be entered into using a credit line provided by the bank since that amounts to selling something you do not own.
- Payment does not have to be in physical cash. Payments over account, cheques, using online banking and so on are equally acceptable as long as the relevant account is in credit.
- Netting of amounts in different currencies between the same parties and settling the net amount is allowed.

The criteria for a foreign exchange contract apply to money in its current form of coins and banknotes, as well as the money-like commodities of the olden days: gold, silver, barley, wheat, dates and salt.

Forward foreign exchange contracts have long been associated with speculation and have long been unacceptable. However, there is a growing recognition that the ability to hedge a forward foreign exchange exposure is not necessarily speculative. Forward foreign exchange contracts are increasingly permitted as long as the contract is entered into for risk-mitigating purposes. Forward contracts are often structured using a unilateral promise described in section 2.5.9.

2.5.9 *Unilateral promise*

A *wa'd* is a unilateral promise from one party to another and can for example be structured along the lines of 'I promise to enter into a spot foreign exchange contract with you in two weeks' time in which I will pay you £2,000 against receiving from you €2,100.' Acceptance by the other party is not required, since this is not a bilateral contract. However, in order for the promise to turn into a contract, offer and acceptance will need to be communicated nearer the date. Although the promisor (the party making the promise) can technically back out, the impact on the party's reputation in the market is severe, which is generally deemed to be a strong deterrent. Similar to English common law, parties can enter into a binding promise, which provides a higher level of certainty.

2.5.10 *Down payment*

An *arbun* represents a non-refundable down payment on a purchase which signifies the buyer's intent to purchase the asset and is typically made toward a good that will be delivered at a later date. The down payment forms part of the overall price agreed between buyer and seller, but is non-refundable in the event the buyer later decides not to take delivery of the asset. Simplified, the steps are as follows:

1. Buyer and seller agree a price and buyer makes a down payment (for example, 20 per cent of the purchase price). The asset is specified and the delivery date is agreed.
2. On the agreed delivery date, the seller delivers the asset to the buyer, or the buyer collects the asset from the seller.
3. On the agreed delivery date, after inspecting the asset, the buyer pays the remaining purchase price (for example, 80 per cent of the original purchase price).

In Islamic finance and *Sharia'a*-compliant fund management, the *arbun* contract can be applied to replicate optionality, although it needs to be taken into consideration that unlike the premium paid for a conventional option, the down payment is part of the total purchase price.

2.5.11 *Bond-like instruments*

Sukuk translates to a legal instrument of deed and is the plural of *sakk* which means cheque or certificate. *Sukuk* are often classified as the Islamic equivalent of a bond, although there are a few differences. From the view point of Islam, conventional bonds have two major drawbacks: they pay interest and there is generally no underlying asset. *Sukuk* are an Islamic security comparable to a conventional covered bond but are not debt instruments. Contrary to conventional bonds, *sukuk* are generally linked to an underlying tangible or intangible asset. Intangible assets are increasingly accepted by scholars, but not yet widely applied. The (beneficial) ownership of the underlying asset is transferred to the holder of the *sukuk* certificates together with all ownership benefits and risks. This gives *sukuk* characteristics of both equity and bonds. *Sukuk* currently issued have a shorter term than conventional bonds and are typically three to five years.

The *sukuk* holder owns a proportional share of the underlying asset, and has a financial right to the revenues generated by the asset. However, as mentioned before, the holder is technically also subject to ownership risk, which means the owner is exposed to any risk and potential losses associated with the share of the underlying asset. Conventional bonds, on the other hand, remain part of the issuer's financial liability.

Sukuk are not a separate financial instrument but are structures facilitating the funding of large projects which would be beyond the capability of either an individual or a small group of investors. *Sukuk* can be listed on recognised exchanges and, with the exception of the *sukuk al salam* and the *sukuk al murabaha,* can be traded in the secondary market. Unlike the conventional bond market, however, *sukuk* tend to be held to maturity and the secondary market is not yet very active. Although quotes are provided by some market makers, the spreads between bid and asking price are particularly wide and availability of issues is currently still thin.

Sukuk can be based on many different transaction types, such as *mudaraba, salam, musharaka* and *ijara,* and the choice of underlying instrument will strongly depend on the ultimate requirement of the originator. The vast majority of *sukuk* currently outstanding is *sukuk al-ijara*, which is based on a sale and lease-back transaction in which the originator sells an existing asset to the issuer, the SPV (special purpose vehicle), and leases it back. The proceeds are subsequently used to finance expansion or other projects.

The generic underlying *sukuk* structure is depicted in Figure 2.5, although it should be noted that variations occur depending on the underlying transaction type. Although the steps could differ for the different structures, the underlying principles remain the same and involve the following steps once the SPV is in place:

1. The corporation sells an asset to the SPV, which the SPV divides up in equal units of usually $1,000 or £1,000 and transfers on to the *sukuk* holders. In the event the underlying transaction is a *musharaka* or *mudaraba* the underlying asset can be represented by a share in the corporation or partnership.

2. The *sukuk* holders transfer the funds representing the number of certificates they bought to the SPV who

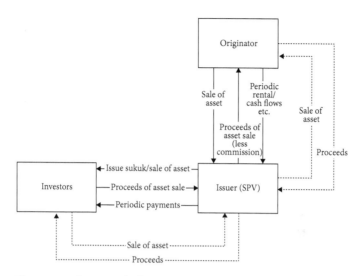

Figure 2.5 *Generic* sukuk *structure*

transfers the total proceeds minus any costs to the corporation.

3. The corporation invests the funds in the *Sharia'a*-compliant investment stipulated in the contract.

4. The *Sharia'a*-compliant investment either generates profits and losses (for partnership-type contracts) or pays a return (for predictable return-type instruments).

5. The SPV collects profits and losses or returns and pays (typically quarterly) coupons to the *sukuk* holder.

6. At maturity, the *sukuk* holder sells the asset to the SPV, who in turn sells it back to the corporation.

7. Money flows from the corporation to the *sukuk* holders through the SPV.

Sukuk are not only originated by corporations, but also by governments and other sovereign entities and public enterprises in which case the 'corporation' in the above structure can be replaced accordingly.

Under the *sukuk* rules as issued by AAOIFI, any *sukuk* must be clearly defined and bankruptcy remote. In addition, any transaction in which ownership of an asset is involved requires a true sale. The only exception to this rule would be in countries where for legal or regulatory reasons it is more efficient to keep the asset on the balance sheet of the issuer of the *sukuk*. In addition, AAOIFI added the following restrictions in February 2008:

1. **Purchase undertaking.** A purchase undertaking by the issuer is typically part of the structure and serves as a guarantee to the *sukuk* holders that their investment will be returned to them at the end of the period. Only in a *sukuk al ijara*, which is based on a sale and lease-back transaction, is it allowed to have a purchase undertaking at a price pre-agreed at the start of the transaction. In *sukuk al mudaraba*, *sukuk al musharaka* and *sukuk al wakala*, a purchase undertaking is allowed, as long as it is executed at the market value of the underlying partnership or asset on the maturity date, and not on a pre-agreed price.

2. *Sukuk* **manager guarantee.** The *sukuk* manager cannot provide a guarantee to make good the shortfall of any income to the *sukuk* holder. Due to the fact that there is no longer a guarantee in case of a default, *sukuk* will rank *pari passu* with ordinary secured debt.

3. **Reserves.** The *sukuk* manager is entitled to build up reserves out of the profit or rentals to cover any potential future shortfall, which partly offsets lack of a guarantee. However, amounts will have to be appropriated to the reserve before distributing the profit to the *sukuk* holders. This provides potential to offer different tranches which will allow investors to invest according to their risk appetite.

The tightening of the rules will result in enhanced *Sharia'a* compliance of *sukuk* issued and increased transparency.

Notes
1. *Oxford Dictionary of Finance and Banking* (1997), 2nd edition (Oxford: Oxford University Press).
2. Ibid.

CHAPTER 3
THE ISLAMIC ASSET MANAGEMENT MARKET PLACE

A large variety of funds exists in the *Sharia'a*-compliant funds market, many with similar investment and return characteristics as conventional funds. This section provides an overview of the different types of fund available, as well as a high-level overview of the Islamic asset management market place at the time of writing. The *Sharia'a*-compliant funds market has evolved significantly over the past years and is expected to continue to develop as new investment opportunities occur and the demand for different types of fund develops. This book provides an overview of the *Sharia'a*-compliant funds that are currently most commonly in existence.

Like conventional investment managers, *Sharia'a*-compliant investment managers can invest in a wide range of products and asset classes including shares and other securities, as long as the individual investments, as well as the overall fund, remain compliant with *Sharia'a*. In addition, in line with the general consensus, Islamic fund managers cannot short sell, speculate, pay or receive interest or apply stock lending techniques, which has an impact on the range of instruments that can be applied.

The *Sharia'a*-compliant fund structures available in the market are typically similar to conventional structures although again *Sharia'a* compliance is a key factor. A *Sharia'a* supervisory board, which is typically made up of three to five members, is involved from the start of the fund, and is typically appointed prior to incorporation. The *Sharia'a* supervisory board is not responsible for any operational and strategic decisions the fund manager makes as long as the fund continues to be *Sharia'a* compliant. The *Sharia'a* supervisory board is, however, involved in the definition of the framework the fund operates in and defines issues such as which industries are deemed compliant. The role of the *Sharia'a* supervisory board in Islamic asset management is detailed in Chapter 6.

The remainder of this chapter will first provide an overview of the Islamic fund management markets, followed by more detailed descriptions of each of the broad fund categories available in the market.

3.1 The Islamic fund market

When Islamic funds were first established in the 1970s, their main purpose was to provide a vehicle to invest in a socially responsible or ethical investment manner, bearing in mind the underlying principles of *Sharia'a*. The funds mainly made direct investments in companies whose operations did not include any non-permissible activities, such as alcohol, gambling or armoury. At the time, it was uncertain whether trading shares was acceptable, and not many products were available in the market beyond direct investments and savings products. From a handful of available funds in the 1970s and 1980s the *Sharia'a*-compliant fund market has grown significantly, mainly because of the development of the industry and the significant increase in the range of available instruments and increased awareness.

The number of *Sharia'a*-compliant funds is increasing

rapidly with new funds being announced on a regular basis. Although most equity funds use some form of benchmark against which to track their performance, the majority of funds appear to have an active management strategy.

As of the end of 2009, the number of funds listed in the Eurekahedge[1] database was nearing 700 with reported assets of just under $50 billion. Taking into consideration the fact that around 20 per cent of the funds do not disclose their assets under management, the total assets is estimated to be around $70 billion. This implies an average size in assets under management of $100 million which, in comparison with the conventional fund market, is particularly small. In comparison, the Lipper[2] database contains in excess of 200,000 funds operating globally

Out of the funds that report their assets under management, the majority hold assets below $50 million. Only very few funds hold assets under management in excess of $500 million, the amount which for conventional funds is deemed to be benchmark size.

The geographical investment mandate of the majority of *Sharia'a*-compliant funds focuses on Asia, the Middle East and Africa or has a global mandate. Most funds have a fairly

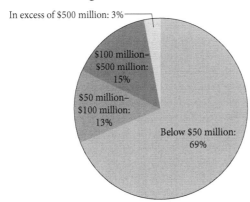

Figure 3.1 *Average assets under management*

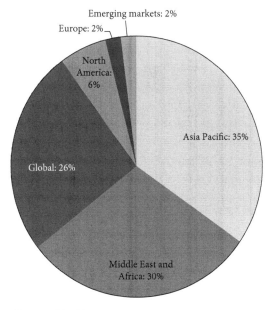

Figure 3.2 *Geographical investment strategy*

wide remit within which they invest. Few funds have specific focus on sub-segments such as the Gulf Cooperation Council (GCC), or individual countries.

In excess of 65 per cent of the funds listed does not specify a particular industry, but reports all industries are in scope of the investment mandate.

Generally, the types of fund offered are similar to the ones offered in the conventional world. The funds are divided into the following broad categories:

1. Fixed income funds
2. Lease funds
3. Commodity funds
4. Equity funds
   a. Private equity

b. Public equity
c. Equity index funds
5. Real estate funds
6. Exchange traded funds
7. Hedge funds

The remainder of this chapter provides further details for each of these types of fund, the assets, different subsections and any other details that may be relevant from a *Sharia'a*-compliance perspective.

3.2 Fixed income funds

Fixed income funds are also known as money market funds and can roughly be divided into five different types based on the risk–return characteristics of the fund itself. As with any fund, higher risk may result in higher return, but can equally result in larger possible losses. It is however not only risk that has an impact on the potential returns: transaction costs, as well as costs associated with maintaining liquidity in a fund, all have an impact on the net return of the fund. A successful fixed income fund, whether *Sharia'a* compliant or not, will make use of the money market instruments at its disposal with an appropriate mix of liquidity, security and return, and can invest in any combination of the following instruments to generate a return on liquid assets:[3]

- **Cash.** Typically some cash balances are held in *Sharia'a*-compliant current accounts to provide the fund manager with the liquidity to meet immediate requirements. Current accounts are interest free and usually do not generate a return by any other means either.
- *Wakala.* Agency agreements can be used to place funds with any other Islamic financial institutions for onward

investment against a return. Under the *wakala* agreement, which is described in further detail in section 2.3.2, the Islamic financial institution acting as agent is free to invest in any opportunity that it deems suitable to generate the best possible return, provided it is *Sharia'a* compliant. Due to the fact that both parties are Islamic financial institutions, there is an implicit guarantee that the investment will be *Sharia'a* compliant.

- **Commodity *murabaha.*** The commodity *murabaha* agreement, which is described in more detail in section 2.3.1, is used in Islamic finance to enable the placement of interbank deposits. Commodity *murabaha* contracts can be entered into with Islamic and non-Islamic institutions alike, as the transaction itself is compliant with *Sharia'a*. Fixed income funds typically use commodity *murabaha* to place funds for relatively short periods against a fixed return.

- **Collective investment schemes.** For longer-dated investments, *Sharia'a*-compliant fund managers have the opportunity to invest in other, *Sharia'a*-compliant collective investment schemes. The type of scheme will be determined by the fund manager in line with the investment mandate and liquidity requirements.

- ***Sukuk.*** Generally, *sukuk* is an instrument that provides a higher yield for the investor in return for taking a higher level of risk. *Sukuk*, described in more detail in section 2.5.11, is a bond-type instrument and is usually held for a longer investment period even though this does not necessarily always have to be the case. *Sukuk* are either purchased directly upon issue from the issuer or from other investors in the secondary market. The secondary market in *sukuk* is at the time of writing still reasonably thin and illiquid, although this part of the market is currently developing in line with other parts of the Islamic finance industry. Investing in *sukuk* is generally deemed to enhance the return profile of a fund.

- **Ijara.** The purchase of, or investment in, a pool of leasing transactions provides a steady return, generally in excess of money market returns against a relatively low risk, particularly where it concerns finance leases, described in detail in section 2.5.6.

The majority of the outperformance of a fixed income fund will be generated by investments in instruments with longer maturities such as *sukuk* and potentially large *ijara* positions. The necessary liquidity in the fund will be generated from the short-term instruments like *wakala* and commodity *murabaha* transactions. The exact allocation of the different instruments in the fund will depend on the framework of the fund, its objectives and the defined risk appetite, as well as the availability of the instruments in the primary and secondary markets and the economic circumstances. In uncertain economic circumstances the amount of redemptions is generally expected to be higher. As a result, the liquidity of the fund will be required to be higher, and as such the investment strategy is likely to shift to a larger proportion of short-term investments.

The asset allocation of a fixed income-type fund defines where the fund would be positioned on the risk–return curve. As a broad rule of thumb, the fixed income funds can be divided into five main types: deposit funds; liquidity funds; money market funds; enhanced cash funds; and high-yield funds. Figure 3.3 indicates how these funds can be compared given their level of risk, expected return and level of liquidity, although in order to achieve higher returns the investment generally has a higher level of risk. On the other hand, higher risk also means the investment may potentially generate a higher loss since the value of investments can go up as well as down. However, funds with a lower level of liquidity typically have higher returns associated with them due to the fact that the money can be invested for a longer period, and returns are smoother over a longer time horizon, even when the day-to-day volatility could potentially be higher.

It is important to note that the names of the funds below or their features are not necessarily similar to those currently available in the market. The funds outlined here provide a generic overview of different fund types in the fixed income funds range.

Deposit funds

The more low-risk, highly liquid and generally low-return deposit funds typically invest in deposit-type instruments with an average maturity of 60 days. The maximum maturity for an individual asset is usually up to one year.

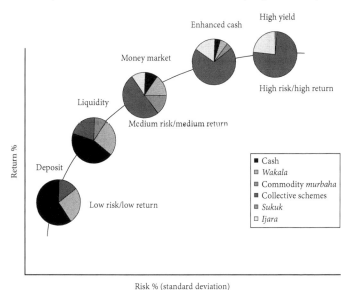

Figure 3.3 *Fixed income funds on the risk–return curve*

Deposit funds have a high level of liquidity and generally allow investors to redeem and subscribe on a daily basis, thus providing the investor with a high level of liquidity. Although the return is relatively low, it is generally in excess of the returns that can be obtained by keeping the funds in a deposit account at a bank. The asset allocation is strongly skewed towards the most conservative assets, such as cash, *wakala* and commodity *murabaha*. Contrary to liquidity funds, deposit funds do not invest in any non-cash-type instruments.

Liquidity funds

Like deposit funds, liquidity funds are relatively low risk, low return and have high levels of liquidity although, as can be seen from Figure 3.3, the risk and return levels are slightly higher with a slightly lower liquidity. Liquidity funds typically invest in deposit-type instruments with a small portion of the funds invested in short-dated *sukuk*. The proportion of the fund invested in *sukuk* is unlikely to exceed 20 per cent. The average maturity of the assets is 60 days, with a maximum maturity of two years for an individual asset. Similar to deposit funds, redemptions and subscriptions are likely to be allowed on a daily basis although there may be limitations to the amount that can be redeemed on a single day.

Money market funds

Moving up on the risk–return curve are the money market funds, which generally have medium risk levels and provide higher levels of return. Money market funds typically invest in a diversified mix of cash, *wakala*, commodity *murabaha*, *sukuk* and *ijara*. The proportion of funds invested in *sukuk* and *ijara* is likely to be up to 50 per cent of the total amount of assets under management. The average maturity of the underlying assets is around one to two years with a maximum maturity of 10 years for an individual asset. Subscriptions and redemptions are still generally daily, although there may be limitations to the amount that can be redeemed on a single day and the settlement period is generally longer, at three to four working days rather than spot (two working days) for liquidity and deposit funds, which provides the fund manager with the possibility of having lower amounts on a current account while still being able to meet the liquidity requirements of the fund and the investors.

Enhanced cash funds

At medium to high risk and hence an increased potential return or loss, an enhanced cash fund typically invests in a diversified mix of cash, *wakala*, and commodity *murabaha* to meet its liquidity requirements and in addition allocates a large proportion of between fifty and eighty per cent to *sukuk* and *ijara* which provides the potential for higher yields. In order to achieve the higher return, the investment horizon is longer with an average maturity of the underlying assets being one to five years with a maximum of ten years for an individual instrument. Subscriptions and redemptions are likely to be daily although there are likely to be limitations to the amounts that can be redeemed on a single day or during a single period, and the average settlement period tends to remain around a period of three to four days, although longer settlement periods are sometimes invoked.

High-yield funds

At the highest risk–return end of the spectrum for fixed income funds are the high-yield funds, which typically invest in a diversified mix of cash, *wakala* and commodity *murabaha*. In order to achieve the desired return, a large proportion of around 80 per cent is typically allocated to investments in *sukuk* and *ijara*. Similar to the enhanced cash fund, the average maturity of the underlying assets is between one and five years with a maximum of ten years for an individual instrument. To further enhance any potential return, the fund manager may invest in instruments which are not in the base currency of the fund and leave part or all of the currency exposure unhedged as part of the investment strategy. Subscriptions and redemption are typically daily, with the average settlement period remaining at three to four working days, although a longer settlement period may be invoked. In order to manage liquidity, the fund manager may put limitations on the amount of money that can be redeemed on a single day or during a certain period.

3.3 Lease funds

Lease-based funds are generally considered to be slightly higher risk and potentially provide a higher return than fixed income funds. The risk levels on a lease fund tend to be higher since the investment has the potential to be less diversified in combination with the ownership risk on the underlying asset. On the other hand, there are a number of advantages to investing in a lease-based fund:

- the fund owns the asset, which is of significance from a *Sharia'a*-compliance perspective;
- the lessee – that is, the user of the asset – relies on the availability of the asset for their operations and is hence less likely to default on the rental payments; and
- finance leases do not take residual risk on the asset, and since the periodic payment includes a principal repayment as well as a rental contribution the cash streams are predictable over the duration of the investment.

Mufti Taqi Usmani, a well-respected Islamic scholar and economist, specifies the following rules for lease funds to be acceptable:

1. The leased assets must have some usufruct, and the rental must be charged only from that point of time when the usufruct is handed over to the lessee.
2. The leased assets must be of a nature that their *halal* (permissible) use is possible.
3. The lessor must undertake all the responsibilities consequent to the ownership of the assets.
4. The rental must be fixed and known to the parties right at the beginning of the contract.

In this type of the fund the management should act as an agent of the subscribers and should be paid a fee for his services. The management fee may be a fixed amount or a proportion of the rentals received. Most of the Muslim jurists are of the view that such a fund cannot be created on the basis of *mudarabah*, because *mudarabah*, according to them, is restricted to the sale of commodities and does not extend to the business of services and leases. However, in the Hanbali school, *mudarabah* can be affected in services and leases also. This view has been preferred by a number of contemporary scholars.[4]

In practice, lease funds typically hold around 10 to 20 per cent of their funds in relatively short-term liquid instruments such as cash, commodity *murabaha* and *wakala* in order to meet their liquidity requirements. In some cases however, the proportions of liquid instruments might be less than that which is likely to be off-set by lower limits of redemptions or longer redemption periods in order for the fund manager to manage the liquidity demands of the investors.

As far as lease investments are concerned, the structure of a lease fund is likely to be, but not necessarily, as depicted in Figure 3.4.

The lease fund collects and manages investor funds and invests these funds in one or more special purpose vehicles. The role of the SPV is to own the leases on behalf of the investors. The SPV could issue certificates to the fund manager or multiple fund managers. The advantage of using an SPV is that the leases as well as the underlying assets are retained by the SPV and only the ownership in the SPV or the certificates it issues changes, which may prevent any potential tax and ownership transfer issues that might otherwise occur depending on the jurisdiction of the lessor.

The SPV, in its role as lessor, purchases the assets and leases them to the lessee. The SPV manages the receipt of periodic rental payments from the lessee and manages any other functions a lessor has. The SPV makes periodic payments to the fund manager as agreed and re-invests the proceeds in any asset category depending on its requirements.

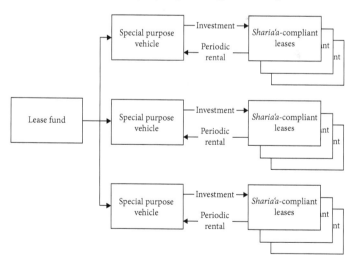

Figure 3.4 *Lease fund structure*

3.4 Commodity funds

In a commodity fund, the fund manager uses the investments in the fund to purchase commodities with the intention to sell them at a profit. The profit is either reinvested or distributed on a pro rata basis to the investors. In order for an investment to be eligible, it needs to fulfil a number of criteria associated with a valid sales contract.

- **Ownership.** The commodity must be owned by the seller at the time of sale. Short selling is not permitted.
- **Forward selling.** Forward sales are not permitted unless the transaction is associated with short- or long-term production finance (*salam* or *istisna).*
- **Acceptability.** The commodity has to be lawful or *halal* and can for instance not be alcohol, pork or any other commodity prohibited in *Sharia'a*.
- **Possession.** The seller must have physical or constructive possession of the commodity, which implies that the ownership risk is with the seller.
- **Price.** The price at which the commodity is sold needs to be certain and unconditional.

The risk of investing in a commodity fund is higher than a lease-based or money market fund due to the fact that the price volatility of the underlying commodities is generally higher. *Sharia'a*-compliant commodity funds typically invest in base metals, precious metals and oil and gas-related commodities.

3.5 Real estate funds

Real estate funds can invest in commercial and residential real estate and generate a yield from rental income and increase in value. Rental income is generally re-invested in the fund or used to repay any mortgage financing. Any property that is purchased for a fund needs to be *Sharia'a* compliant, and its uses will be monitored for ongoing compliance. Commercial properties that are leased to conventional financial institutions, or any other unlawful industries, cannot be included in the fund. Given the multiple use of many properties, the fund mandate typically allows a small percentage of up to 5 per cent of use to be non-compliant although any income associated with the non-compliant use will need to be donated to charity. In the event the non-compliant use increases, the property will have to be disposed of in an organised manner. Generally a reasonable period of time is allowed for the disposal process in line with market conditions so as to not disadvantage the investors.

3.6 Equity funds

Investing in equity, whether private equity, direct investments, public equity or index trackers, attracts the highest levels of risk of all investments described previously and has the potential to generate large returns as well as large potential losses. Equity, and in particular direct investments, fit well with the principles of *Sharia'a*. Not only does it have the potential to create wealth for the investor, it also enables others to increase their wealth, creates jobs and is generally of benefit to the overall economy. Islamic investors cannot, however, invest in any industries that are deemed to be *haram*, or unlawful. The remainder of this section will look in detail at the selection criteria that are applied to ensure the investment is *Sharia'a* compliant, the different options to invest in equity using *Sharia'a*-compliant funds and the available benchmarks.

3.6.1 *Selecting* Sharia'a-*compliant equity*

The Accounting and Auditing Organization for Islamic Financial Institutions (AAOIFI) has defined two screening criteria for the selection of *Sharia'a*-compliant equity. The criteria for both screens need to be met in order for an equity to be allowable. The screening process first determines whether or not the industry itself complies, and then applies financial criteria in order to ascertain whether or not the company is excessively leveraged, holds too much of its assets in cash, or generates a more than insignificant amount of its income from interest or prohibited activities. The screening criteria outlined in this section are those defined in AAOIFI *Sharia'a* standard 21.

Industry screen

The first selection when deciding whether to accept a share in the investment universe is often referred to as the 'industry screen'. Although it is preferable to allow only fully *Sharia'a*-compliant funds in the universe, increasing globalisation, diversification and market demand do not always make this possible. As a result, a particular share or business can be a *Sharia'a*-compliant investment opportunity, even when an insignificant amount of the turnover is deemed to be *haram* or unlawful. Although the definition of 'insignificant' varies between *Sharia'a* supervisory boards and individual investors, it is generally accepted to be 5 per cent or less of total turnover.

The industry screen is meant to eliminate any unlawful businesses from the investment universe and aims to exclude any industries or sectors that should not form part of the portfolio of any Islamic investor. The following industries are generally prohibited:

- **Conventional banking and insurance.** There are multiple reasons for conventional banking and insurance companies to be prohibited, such as the fact that they pay and receive interest as part of their operations and are associated with speculative transactions. In addition, conventional banks tend to issue preference shares, which are not permissible due to the fact that they pay a fixed dividend and are therefore comparable with interest-bearing debt.
- **Alcohol.** The prohibition on alcohol is far reaching and extends to distilling, marketing and sale. It also includes working in the industry: distillers, brewers, pubs and any business that generates a significant amount of its revenue from the sale or production of alcohol. Medicinal alcohol and alcohol used in the production of perfumes, however, is exempt from this prohibition.
- **Pork-related products and non-compliant food production.** Besides the production, selling and marketing of all pork foods, the prohibition extends to all foods whose preparation is not *halal* and covers, among others, meat which is not slaughtered in an acceptable fashion.
- **Gambling.** Any industry involved in gambling and speculation including, but not restricted to, casinos, betting shops, bingo halls and online betting is prohibited within *Sharia'a* without any exception.
- **Tobacco.** Similar to the prohibition on alcohol, the prohibition on tobacco is wider than just the involvement in production and includes the marketing and sales thereof as well as associated products such as, for example, cigarettes and cigars.
- **Adult entertainment.** Any activity associated with adult entertainment including escort services, brothels and films with explicit sexual content is prohibited. Although some scholars extend this prohibition to include films

in general, the AAOIFI standard solely prohibits adult entertainment.

- **Weapons, arms and defence manufacturing.** The production, sale and marketing of weaponry and armoury extends to include other defence-related items.

The industry screen outlined in the above list provides a consensus view among most schools of thought on the industries that should not be permitted. In practice, however, it can be observed that differences of opinion exist between schools of thought and even between individual scholars on the acceptability of certain industries. Some scholars for example permit tobacco and related industries whereas others extend the adult entertainment industry to the wider entertainment industry to include, among others, hotels and the film industry.

Financial screen

Once the industry screen has determined which companies remain part of the investment universe on the basis of their operational activities, a financial screen is applied which specifically considers issues such as conventional leverage, a company's cash position and income from non-compliant operations.

The financial screen defined in AAOIFI *Sharia'a* standard 21 provides the financial ratios based on the consensus view among scholars. Although the exact financial ratios can vary, the generally accepted financial ratios are outlined below.

Conventional debt ratio

Any company with conventional debt in excess of 30 per cent of conventional debt is excluded from the investment universe. In other words, in order to be included in the investment universe, a company needs to meet the following criteria:

$$\frac{\text{Conventional debt}}{\text{Total assets}} < 30\%$$

Cash and deposit ratio

Any company for which the total cash plus interest-bearing deposits is in excess of 30 per cent is excluded from the investment universe.

$$\frac{(\text{Cash} + \text{interest-bearing deposits})}{\text{Total assets}} < 30\%$$

Interest-bearing deposits are included in this ratio because of the prohibition on interest, although it is recognised that internationally operating companies may have an element of interest received. Cash is included in this ratio since excessive cash balances are deemed to equate to hoarding, which is prohibited within *Sharia'a*. In addition, holding excessive cash is generally seen as a sign that the company is not able to generate returns in excess of the cost of capital and is hence not re-investing, and there is an expectation that companies with excessive cash balances are more likely to overpay for an investment. Companies with excessive cash balances often consider strategic alternatives such as buying back shares for these reasons.

Interest and non-compliant income ratio

It is generally recognised that a small amount of interest or non-*Sharia'a*-compliant income cannot be avoided at all times in internationally active companies. It is therefore accepted that an insignificant part of the firm's revenue may be non-compliant as per the following ratio:

$$\frac{(\text{Total interest} + \text{income from non-compliant activities})}{\text{Total revenue}} < 5\%$$

The *Sharia'a*-compliant fund manager will have to purify any proportion of the dividend that is attributable to the non-compliant income by giving it away to charity. When the fund purifies the funds on behalf of the investor, it is generally the *Sharia'a* supervisory board that decides to which charities the amounts will be donated. The fund's *Sharia'a* supervisory board also verifies the amounts that need to be purified.

Similar to the industry screening standards, the financial standards outlined in this section, which are defined in AAOIFI *Sharia'a* standard 21, provide a consensus view among the schools of thought on the financial ratios and their components. Different *Sharia'a*-compliant funds can therefore apply variations on the ratios defined above and it is up to the individual investor to ensure they are comfortable with the ratios implemented by the fund.

The screening process in Sharia'a-compliant equity funds
The industry screen and financial screens outlined in the previous sections are those that are defined in AAOIFI *Sharia'a* standard 21, and that provide a consensus view among the various schools of thought in Islam regarding the acceptability of certain industries and the levels of conventional debt financing, cash and non-compliant deemed appropriate. As pointed out previously, there are differences of opinion between schools of thought and even between individual scholars on the acceptability of the screening criteria. Some scholars for example permit tobacco and related industries whereas others extend the adult entertainment industry to the wider entertainment industry to include, among others, hotels and the film industry. Concerning

the financial screens, some scholars allow a third (that is, 33.33 per cent) of conventional debt as a proportion of total assets. These differences also clearly shown in the construction of *Sharia'a*-compliant indices, further described in section 3.6.5.

Based on their own interpretation, individual investors could again have their own view on the acceptability of an industry within their portfolio and have a different opinion on the financial ratios. Equally *Sharia'a*-compliant equity funds do not necessarily need to abide by the same AAOIFI *Sharia'a* standard outlined above, but can apply their own rules regarding acceptability of industries and financial ratios. It is important to bear in mind that the AAOIFI standard can be used as a consensus guideline, but is by no means rigid or the only acceptable standard. For investors in a *Sharia'a*-compliant equity fund it is therefore of the utmost importance to satisfy themselves that the industry screen used by the fund is acceptable to them.

3.6.2 Private equity

Slightly below 50 per cent of the funds listed in the Eurekahedge database at the end of 2009 list 'equities' as the instruments they trade. Many of these are equity trackers or invest in listed equity, and only very few might invest in private equity, venture capital or direct investments.

The European Private Equity and Venture Capital Association (EVCA) defines private equity as follows:

> Private equity provides equity capital to enterprises not quoted on a stock market. Private equity can be used to develop new products and technologies (also called venture capital), to expand working capital, to make acquisitions, or to strengthen a company's balance sheet. It can also resolve ownership and management issues. A succession in family-owned companies,

or the buyout and buyin [*sic*] of a business by experienced managers may be achieved by using private equity funding.[5]

Investing in private equity is generally perceived as a high-risk investment strategy, largely because many companies are in the early phase of their development, are relatively small in size, and are closely linked to the state of the local economy.

From a *Sharia'a*-compliant investor's perspective, the advantage of private equity investments is that they are more likely to have lower conventional debt levels, and hence will more easily pass the financial screen detailed in section 3.6.1. In addition, compared with large, internationally operating companies, local private equity (that is, those companies incorporated and focussed on a geographical area that is predominantly populated by Muslims) is more likely to be *Sharia'a* compliant. Furthermore, investing in local private equity would have a positive *Sharia'a* impact, since it focuses on the economic well-being of the direct community. Its closeness to the local community in combination with the, generally, relatively small size of the investment is also one of the main disadvantages of private equity investing. The volatility of these investments is generally higher due to the strong interaction with, and reliance, on the local economy. Diversification can be achieved by investing in funds rather than directly, but it has to be considered that private equity investing is labour intensive for the fund manager, which is typically reflected in a higher management fee.

3.6.3 *Public equity*

The investment in publicly listed equity is permissible as long as the screening criteria outlined in section 3.6.1, or those approved by the investor or the fund's *Sharia'a* supervisory board, are met. The acceptability of companies that obtain less than 5 per cent of their revenues from non-*Sharia'a*-compliant activities is justified in light of the fact that in a global economy it would be difficult, if not impossible, to identify any company that is fully *Sharia'a* compliant in both its activities and its modes of financing.

The investors in the equity fund are identified as partners in the fund, and the investment amounts are pooled to facilitate the purchase of shares. As alluded to previously, any non-*Sharia'a*-compliant investment due to the fund investor will need to be purified by donating it to charity. There are different ways to achieve this:

1. The fund's *Sharia'a* supervisory board determines the amount of income that needs to be purified and determines which charities will be the beneficiaries. This typically occurs for funds where income is re-invested or where the fund manager deducts the purified amount from the distribution to the investors.
2. The fund's *Sharia'a* supervisory board determines the amount of income that needs to be purified and informs the investors who in turn take responsibility for making the donations to charities of their choice. This typically occurs when periodical distributions are made to the investors' gross of any charitable contributions.

The general consensus among scholars is that both dividend income and capital gains need to be purified to reflect the income attributable to non *Sharia'a*-compliant activities.

The performance of funds investing in public equity is typically measured against any one of the *Sharia'a*-compliant indices which serves as a benchmark. The variety of *Sharia'a*-compliant indices has grown exponentially in line with the market and they are described in further detail in section 3.6.5.

3.6.4 Index tracker funds

Index tracker funds are collective investment vehicles designed to follow or track the performance of a particular index. The out- or underperformance of the fund in comparison to its benchmark is measured by the tracking error.[6] In its simplest form, tracking the index would involve buying every share in the index at the exact weight in the index and rebalancing as individual weights change or companies are added and removed from the index. The problems with this approach are:

1. The weight is not in round shares, and purchasing a part share is not possible.
2. The volume of transactions required to track the index this way would be unnecessarily high and lead to high transaction costs which would in turn result in (potentially significant) underperformance of the fund.

Instead, index tracker funds typically apply sophisticated statistical modelling techniques, such as partial replication, which will provide them with a portfolio with a lower number of holdings and a very high probability of performing exactly like the index. As a result of the lower number of holdings, the transaction cost will also be significantly reduced.

The main advantages of index trackers are that they are relatively cheap to operate whilst providing a diversified exposure to the overall market. The fund manager's fees are typically low, although the potential for outperformance of the index is equally relatively low.

Some fund managers provide a potential opportunity for outperformance via enhanced indexing, in which case the fund is an index tracker combined with an element of active investment – that is, the fund manager picks their own shares based on their view of the market and other technical analysis techniques without any reference to the index.

Until the advent of *Sharia'a*-compliant indices, *Sharia'a*-compliant index tracking funds used to benchmark their performance against conventional indices with an adjustment for non-*Sharia'a*-compliant shares and revenues. This unfortunate situation came to an end when the conventional index providers such as Dow Jones Indexes, FTSE and MSCI started to construct *Sharia'a*-compliant indices, which are now generally used as a benchmark for *Sharia'a*-compliant index funds as well as the measurement of the performance of other *Sharia'a*-compliant equity funds.

In order to meet ongoing liquidity requirements, the fund will invest a small proportion, typically of up to 20 per cent, in short-term liquid instruments such as cash, *wakala* or commodity *murabaha*.

3.6.5 Sharia'a-*compliant indices*

As of the start of 2010, all major index providers offer a suite of *Sharia'a*-compliant indices in addition to their conventional offering. The methodology and screening criteria for each of these are outlined in the remainder of this section.

Although there is no significant deviation, for each of the indices both the acceptable business and the acceptable financial ratios differ slightly from the industry and financial screens defined in section 3.6.1. It is important to bear in mind that these differences exist, and individual investors as well as the fund managers will need to satisfy themselves that the criteria applied are acceptable to them.

FTSE Shariah Global Equity Index Series

The FTSE Global Islamic Index Series was originally introduced in late 1998 and has since been expanded upon and replaced by the FTSE Shariah Global Equity Index Series, in 2007. The FTSE Shariah Global Equity Index Series provides a suite of *Sharia'a*-compliant indices covering a wide range of indices including countries and regions[7].

The series uses the FTSE Global Equity Index Series as the base investment universe and applies business activity and financial ratio screening. It is affiliated with *Sharia'a* consultancy that acts as its *Sharia'a* supervisory board. The index series applies the following screening mechanisms:

Business activity screening
The FTSE Shariah Global Equity Index Series excludes any companies that generate their income from conventional finance, alcohol, pork-related products and non-*halal* food production, packaging and processing or any other activity related to pork and non-*halal* foods, and entertainment including, but not restricted to, casinos, gambling and pornography, tobacco, and weapons, arms and defence manufacturing.

Financial ratio screening
The companies remaining after the industry screen is completed are filtered using the following financial ratios:

1. $\dfrac{\text{Total debt}}{\text{Total assets}} < 33\%$

2. $\dfrac{(\text{Cash} + \text{interest-bearing items})}{\text{Total assets}} < 33\%$

3. $\dfrac{(\text{Accounts receivable} + \text{cash})}{\text{Total assets}} < 50\%$

4. $\dfrac{(\text{Total interest} + \text{non-compliant activities income})}{\text{Total revenue}} < 5\%$

To ensure ongoing compliance of the different indices they are reviewed on a quarterly basis after which any required changes will be implemented.

Dow Jones Islamic Market Indexes
The Dow Jones Islamic Market Indexes (DJIM) were introduced in early 1999 and have evolved ever since to include
multiple indices by country, region, industry and sector with
all of the latter being a subset of the Dow Jones Islamic Market
World Index. The Dow Jones Islamic Market Indexes have
their own *Sharia'a* supervisory board which advises for the
full suite of indices on the methodology used for screening
securities for inclusion in the index and has ongoing responsibility to ensure the indices remain *Sharia'a* compliant.

Selection of the constituents of the index is based on the
Dow Jones World Index as a starting point and applies a set
of screening criteria approved by Dow Jones Indexes' dedicated *Sharia'a* supervisory board. The screening criteria
applied by DJIM Indexes are described below.[8]

Acceptable business activities
Companies that generate in excess of 5 per cent of their
income from alcohol, tobacco, pork-related products, conventional financial services such as banking and insurance,
weapons and defence, and entertainment including, but not
restricted to, hotels, casinos, gambling, cinema, pornography and music, are excluded from the investable universe.
Any company that generates more than 5 per cent of its
income from any of the sectors of the Industry Classification
Benchmark (ICB) identified in table 3.1 is excluded from the
index.

Companies classified as financial in the ICB (code range
8000) are deemed eligible for inclusion in the index if they
are incorporated as an Islamic financial institution such
as Islamic banks and *takaful* companies. In the same vein,
companies classified as real estate (8600) are considered
eligible if the company's operations and properties are
conducting business within *Sharia'a* principles.

ISLAMIC ASSET MANAGEMENT

Table 3.1 *Dow Jones Islamic Market Indexes industry screen*

Code	Description	Code	Description
2717	Defence	5757	Restaurants and bars
3533	Brewers	8355	Banks
3535	Distillers and vintners	8532	Full line insurance
3577	Food products	8534	Insurance brokers
3745	Recreational products	8536	Property and casualty insurance
3785	Tobacco	8538	Reinsurance
5337	Food retailers and wholesalers	8575	Life insurance
5553	Broadcasting and entertainment	8773	Consumer finance
5555	Media agencies	8775	Specialty finance
5752	Gambling	8777	Investment services
5753	Hotels	8779	Mortgage finance
5755	Recreational services		

Acceptable financial ratios

The companies remaining after the industry screen is complete are filtered using the following financial ratios:

1.
$$\frac{\text{Total debt}}{\text{Trailing 24-month average market capitalisation}} < 33\%$$

2.
$$\frac{\text{(Cash + interest-bearing securities)}}{\text{Trailing 24-month average market capitalisation}} < 33\%$$

3.
$$\frac{\text{Accounts receivable}}{\text{Trailing 24-month average market capitalisation}} < 33\%$$

The use of a trailing 24-month average market capitalisation reduces volatility in the denominator. This smoothes the market cap over the recent time period so that companies are not immediately removed from the index if their stock price is effected by transitory extreme declines in market

76

conditions, such as those caused by the sub-prime mortgage crisis. Changes in market capitalisation are, after all, not necessarily the result of a change in operations, but are more likely due to a change in general market conditions.

To ensure ongoing compliance of the different indices they are reviewed on a quarterly basis after which any required changes will be implemented. In addition to the quarterly monitoring, the constituents are also reviewed on an ongoing basis for extraordinary events such as delisting, bankruptcy, mergers and takeovers. Any newly listed securities are evaluated using the same screening process and added to the index when appropriate.

On a quarterly basis Dow Jones provides a report containing impure ratios which can be used by the fund managers as a guideline for purifying dividend income in their fund.

S&P Shariah Indices
Standard and Poor's (S&P) launched the first of its S&P Shariah Indices in 2006 and uses the investable universe of its major conventional indices as a starting point and excludes any stock that is not compliant with *Sharia'a*. Standard and Poor's has affiliated with an advisory company with its own *Sharia'a* supervisory board to define the *Sharia'a* screens. A variety of indices is available by geographical region.[9]

Business Activity Screening
The S&P Shariah Indices exclude the following business activities:

- Pork
- Alcohol
- Gambling
- Financials

- Advertising and media, except newspapers (sub-industries are analysed individually)
- Pornography
- Tobacco
- Trading of gold and silver as cash on deferred basis

Accounting-based screening

The companies remaining after the business activity screening is completed are filtered using the following financial ratios:

1. **Leverage compliance**

$$\frac{\text{Debt}}{\text{Market value of equity (12-month average)}} \quad <33\%$$

2. **Cash compliance**

$$\frac{\text{(Cash + interest-bearing securities)}}{\text{Market value of equity (12-month average)}} \quad <33\%$$

$$\frac{\text{Accounts receivable}}{\text{Market value of equity (12-month average)}} \quad <50\%$$

3. **Revenue share from non-compliant activities**

$$\frac{\text{Non-permissible income other than interest income}}{\text{Revenue}} \quad <5\%$$

To ensure ongoing compliance of the different indices they are reviewed on a quarterly basis after which any required changes will be implemented.

Periodically a dividend purification ratio is provided to investors for purification purposes which is calculated using the following formula:

$$Dividends \quad \frac{Non\text{-}permissible\ revenue}{Total\ revenue}$$

The resulting number can be used by the fund manager to determine the amount of dividend that will be donated to charity prior to reinvestment.

MSCI Islamic Index Series

The MSCI Islamic Index Series was launched in 2007 and uses the investment universe of the equivalent MSCI Equity Index as a basis and applies filtering criteria to determine the constituents of the MSCI Islamic Index. A variety of indices are part of the series including country, region and industry-specific indices.[10]

MSCI has its own *Sharia'a* supervisory board to ensure initial and ongoing *Sharia'a* compliance. The index series applies the following screening mechanisms:

Business activity screening

The MSCI indices exclude companies that are directly active in, or derive in excess of 5 per cent of their revenue (cumulatively) from, any of the following industries:

- **Alcohol.** Distillers, vintners and producers of alcoholic beverages, including producers of beer and malt liquors, owners and operators of bars and pubs.
- **Tobacco.** Cigarettes and other tobacco products manufacturers and retailers.
- **Pork-related products.** Companies involved in the manufacture and retail of pork products.
- **Conventional financial services.** Any company involved in conventional banking, insurance or other interest-related financial services.
- **Defence and weapons.** Manufacturers of military aerospace and defence equipment, parts or products, including defence electronics and space equipment.
- **Gambling and casinos.** Owners and operators of casinos

and gaming facilities, including companies providing lottery and betting services.

- **Music.** Producers and distributors of music, owners and operators of radio broadcasting systems.
- **Hotels.** Owners and operators of hotels excluding revenue from hotel premises operating in Saudi Arabia.
- **Cinema.** Companies engaged in the production, distribution and screening of films and television shows, owners and operators of television broadcasting systems and providers of cable or satellite television services.
- **Adult entertainment.** Owners and operators of adult entertainment products and activities.

Financial ratio screening

The companies remaining after the industry screen is complete are filtered using the following financial ratios:

1. $$\frac{\text{Total debt}}{\text{Total assets}} \qquad <33.33\%$$

2. $$\frac{(\text{Cash} + \text{interest-bearing securities})}{\text{Total assets}} \qquad <33.33\%$$

3. $$\frac{(\text{Accounts receivable} + \text{cash})}{\text{Total assets}} \qquad <33.33\%$$

To ensure ongoing compliance of the different indices they are rebalanced annually and reviewed on a quarterly basis after which any required changes will be implemented.

Any income derived from non-compliant activities is purified by applying a 'dividend adjustment factor' to all reinvested dividends which is defined as follows, where total earnings are defined as gross income, and interest income includes both operating and non-operating interest:

$$\frac{\text{Total earnings} - (\text{income from prohibited activities} + \text{interest income})}{\text{Total earnings}}$$

Russell-Jadwa Shariah Index
The most recent addition to the range of *Sharia'a*-compliant indices is the Russell-Jadwa Shariah Global Index, launched in 2009. Russell-Jadwa consists of a suite of indices mainly grouped by geographical area. It uses the Russell Global Index Universe as the underlying investable universe and has its own *Sharia'a* supervisory board that determines the screening criteria and oversees the screening process. The Russell-Jadwa Shariah Index applies the following screening criteria:

Sector-based screens
Any company whose activities are any of the below is excluded from the index.

- financial institutions such as traditional banks that deal with interest or financial instruments that violate *Sharia'a* rules, traditional insurance companies
- production and distribution of alcohol
- production and distribution of tobacco
- production and distribution of meat not slaughtered according to *Sharia'a* rules
- production and distribution of pork and its derivatives
- management of casinos, gambling halls and production of games such as slot machines
- house of prostitution or vice
- production and distribution of pornographic films, books and magazines, satellite channels and cinemas
- restaurants, hotels and places of entertainment that provide prohibited services such as the sale of alcohol

- trading of gold and silver as cash on deferred basis
- weapon manufacturing and selling
- stem cell/human embryo, genetic cloning (research firms, therapy clinics, and so on)
- anything not *Sharia'a* compliant as determined by the Russell-Jadwa Shariah Board.

Financial-based screens
The companies remaining after the industry screen is complete are filtered using the following financial ratios, each of which needs to be met:

1. $$\frac{\text{(Cash deposits + receivables)}}{\text{12-month total market capitalisation}} \quad <70\%$$

2. $$\frac{\text{Total interest-bearing debt}}{\text{12-month total market capitalisation}} \quad <33\%$$

3. $$\frac{\text{(Cash + deposits + interest-bearing securities)}}{\text{12-month total market capitalisation}} \quad <33\%$$

4. $$\frac{\text{(Interest earned + revenue from prohibited activities)}}{\text{(Total income)}} <5\%$$

Total income is in this case defined as total revenue or sales.

To ensure ongoing compliance of the different indices they are rebalanced annually and reviewed on a quarterly basis after which any required changes will be implemented.

Any income derived from interest-bearing or non-compliant activities is reported using a purification ratio which is determined applying the following process:

The purification process will be as follows:

1. Determine the amount of impure income for an index member by dividing the amount of impure income of

the security by the total number of float adjusted shares to obtain the stock share of the impure income.

2. Multiply the proceeds by the number of float adjusted shares of the index member for the purpose of calculation of the total impure income.

3. Repeat the same steps for each index member.

4. Add the amount of the impure income for all index members.

5. Report the total amount of impure income for the index to the Sharia'a Board for review and approval annually. This approved amount will also be posted for the public on Russell.com. Additionally, daily calculated net and total index values and returns will be purified daily using the purification ratio.

The financial data used in the purification process, including a company's net revenue, net interest income, and revenue from prohibited activities, will be primarily based on the most recent available data, within the preceding two (2) calendar quarters, from an independent, recognized financial data vendor. If this financial data is unavailable, non-financial data sources including analyst research reports may be utilized. Estimated proportions – based on industry or market norms – may be used where financial data is not readily available.[11]

The reported purification ratio can subsequently be used by the fund manager to determine the amount of dividend that will be donated to charity prior to reinvestment.

Sharia'a-compliant indices in brief
Each of the index series described in the preceding sections applies industry and financial ratios which differ slightly, but not significantly, from the screening criteria outlined earlier in section 3.6.1. There is broad agreement on the

industries to be included although some of the indices are stricter on the inclusion of the entertainment industry than the AAOIFI *Sharia'a* standard. The financial ratios differ more widely although even there the differences are not significant. The use of total assets versus market capitalisation in the denominator of the financial ratios is mainly related to the construction of the underlying index. All indices provide a ratio that can be used by the fund manager to determine the proportion of the dividend it has received associated with non-compliant income which needs to be purified by donating it to charity prior to reinvesting.

From an investor's and fund manager's perspective, it is important to bear in mind that these differences exist, and that they need to satisfy themselves that the criteria applied and the choice of index reflects their own values.

3.6.6 Non-compliance

No matter how thorough the screening process, a situation could occur where a private or public equity investment becomes (temporarily) non-compliant which could for example occur as a result of a drastic change in market capitalisation or a merger. It is the responsibility of the fund manager to report this to the *Sharia'a* supervisory board together with a recommendation on how to proceed. Depending on the investment strategy, investment mandate, and whether there is an expectation that the investment will come back to compliance, there are two main courses of action that can be taken in the event non-compliance occurs. Either a process of disinvestment is started directly or the investment is monitored over a period of time to see whether it is coming back to compliance. The majority of funds in the market have opted to only disinvest immediately if the investment is unlikely to come back to compliance, for example because it has changed its business model or has significantly increased its conventional debt as part of a financial strategy. Typically, an investment that has become non-compliant is monitored for a period of time until a final decision on disinvestment is made. Some funds however are required to start the disinvestment process immediately when an investment becomes non-compliant.

Generally, if an investment is deemed to be temporarily non-compliant and it is within the fund's investment guidelines not to immediately disinvest, the *Sharia'a* supervisory board could allow the stock to remain part of the investment universe. The fund manager reports the investment to the *Sharia'a* supervisory board as soon as it becomes non-compliant and monitors and reports its progress over time. All income from the stock during that period will need to be purified by donating it to charity for as long as the non-compliance occurs.

An investment that is unlikely to come back to compliance will require disinvestment. Typically the *Sharia'a* supervisory board will allow disinvestment to take place over a certain period in order to protect investor interests. Once an investment returns to compliance, the fund manager may include it in the investment universe again, although in the decision-making process they are likely to incorporate the fact that an investment was non-compliant and the likelihood of this occurring again.

3.7 Exchange traded funds

Exchange traded funds (ETFs) are securities that track an index, commodity or basket of assets in the same way an index fund does, but trade on an exchange, similar to a stock. ETFs trade during the day and as a result are generally more liquid than other fund types and are subject to price changes during the day as units are traded continuously. As an ETF trades on an exchange, daily net asset value (NAV) calculations are typically not required.

From an investor's perspective, the advantage of holding a position in an ETF lies in the fact that it offers diversification and can easily be bought and sold in any unit size, typically at a lower expense then investing in a comparable fund. Conventional ETFs can be sold short, or traded at a margin.

From a *Sharia'a* compliance perspective, ETFs can provide an opportunity for diversification of an investor's holdings as long as the assets that are underlying the fund are *Sharia'a* compliant.

3.8 Hedge funds

Hedging is the practice of attempting to reduce risk by taking measures such as diversification. The underlying purpose of a hedge fund is to be a risk diversifier and to reduce risk when combined with stock and bond investments. Risk is diversified by the application of short selling and derivatives. Although the aim of the first hedge funds, established in the late 1940s, was to hedge against the downside risk of a bear market by shorting the market, these days the goal of most hedge funds is to maximise return on investment by making speculative investments that generally carry more risk than the overall market.

Hedge funds are generally defined as investment funds open to a limited range of investors which undertake a range of investment and trading activities that go beyond the long-only investment funds. Hedge funds typically invest in a broad range of investments including shares, debts and commodities and generally apply a long–short strategy. More recently, the term hedge fund has been applied to funds that use the same investment strategies to increase rather than to reduce risk and are aggressively managed using leverage, long, short and derivatives positions with the goal being to generate excessive returns either in an absolute sense or in excess of a specific market benchmark.

In most jurisdictions, hedge funds are only open to a limited range of professional or wealthy investors that meet the criteria set by the regulators in the jurisdiction of incorporation. Beyond the regulations governing the investors, hedge funds are typically exempt from many other regulations governing investment funds such as restrictions on short selling, the use of derivatives and leverage. Hedge funds are normally structured as private investment partnerships and require large initial investments and, due to the relative illiquidity, a long initial subscription period of typically one year or more.

Within *Sharia'a*, to sell an asset that the seller does not own, as well as speculation, are prohibited, which would imply that a *Sharia'a*-compliant hedge fund would not be a possibility. Yet hedging excessive risk is deemed to be prudent. Over the past few years there have been a number of attempts at setting up *Sharia'a*-compliant hedge funds, some more successful than others, but none of them have managed to attract a significant amount of investments so far. *Sharia'a* scholars have to date not reached a consensus view on the acceptability of hedge funds, although some instruments for short selling have been permitted using *salam, arbun* and *wa'd* contracts or a combination of these. Examples of these contracts are as follows:

1. **Salam.** A *salam* contract can be applied to replicate an uncovered short sale of equity. The payment for the shares is made in full on the contract trade date whilst delivery of the shares is delayed to a future date. Although permitted by some *Sharia'a* scholars, AAOIFI specifically

links *salam* to commodities and therefore deems the use of *salam* to short sell equities as not permitted.

2. **Wa'd.** Unilateral promises or *wa'd* can be applied to replicate a covered short sale position by exchanging two unilateral promises, one by the short seller and one by the lending party. A potential structure could for example be as follows:

   - *Wa'd* 1 – Islamic fund promises a prime broker to sell him a number of shares in a specified company on or before a specified future date, at a given price level if the price is in excess of the current price.
   - *Wa'd* 2 – Prime broker promises to buy the same number of shares in the same company on or before a specified future date, at a given price level if the price is below the current price. The purchase price in this promise is different from the price agreed in *wa'd* 1.

   Sharia'a compliance is achieved as a result of the fact that the promises are unilateral and the agreed purchase and sale price differ.

3. **Arbun.** A down payment or *arbun* can be used to replicate either a short sale or optionality in a contract. The buyer makes a down payment on the purchase of shares and pays the remaining of the agreed purchase price upon delivery of the shares on an agreed future date. The purchaser does not have to take delivery of the full number of shares, although they will in that case forfeit the down payment.

Any combination of the above contracts could be structured to achieve a *Sharia'a*-compliant short sale or optionality. However, the opinions on acceptability of these contracts vary widely between different geographical locations and different schools of thought. For example, whereas the Malaysian *Sharia'a* council approves the use of most of the above-mentioned structures for the purpose of replicating short selling techniques, the Accounting and Auditing Organization for Islamic Financial Institutions restricts the use of *salam* contracts to commodities only, basically rendering the contract unacceptable for shares.[12]

Notes

1. Eurekahedge is a subscription-only database provider which collates and publishes data on hedge funds, private equity funds and a number of specialist funds including *Sharia'a* compliant ones. Individual share classes are incorporated as a separate entry. http://www.eurekahedge.com/specialfunds/index.asp

2. Lipper, which is a Thompson Reuters Company, provides a subscription-only service listing conventional funds.

3. As the market develops, other instruments can be considered for inclusion.

4. http://www.albalagh.net/Islamic_economics/finance.shtml

5. http://www.evca.eu/toolbox/glossary.aspx?id=3178&terms =private+equity+definition

6. Tracking error is a measurement to determine how much the return on a portfolio deviates from the return on the benchmark index, and is represented by the standard deviation of the difference between the portfolio and the benchmark using the following formula:

$$\sigma^2 = 1/(n-1) \; \Sigma(x_i - y_i)^2$$

Where σ is the tracking error
n is the number of periods over which it is measured
x is the percentage return on the portfolio in period i
y is the percentage return on the benchmark.

7. http://www.ftse.com

8. Guide to the Dow Jones Islamic Market Indexes, December 2009.

9. http://www.standardandpoors.com
10. http://www.mscibarra.com
11. Russell-Jadwa Shariah Index Summary Methodology, June 2009.
12. AAOIFI *Sharia'a* standard 10.

CHAPTER 4
FUND OPERATIONS

Sharia'a-compliant funds are often registered in Western jurisdictions that have established regulatory frameworks that apply to all funds, whether conventional or *Sharia'a* compliant. In addition, *Sharia'a*-compliant funds are typically distributed internationally and hence are required by investors to follow internationally accepted procedures in their dealings with clearers, brokers, fund managers and investors. The operational structure outlined in this chapter is not specific to any type of fund, but describes a generic operational structure. The remainder of this chapter starts with a generic structure of an asset management firm or division, followed by a description of the different parties and their roles.

4.1 Asset management company structure

Funds have a variety of associated parties, which vary marginally depending on the type and the jurisdiction in which they are based. A generic structure is defined in Figure 4.1, which demonstrates that the structure of *Sharia'a*-compliant asset management is almost identical to that of its conventional equivalent but with one major difference. In order to ensure *Sharia'a* compliance of the funds, a

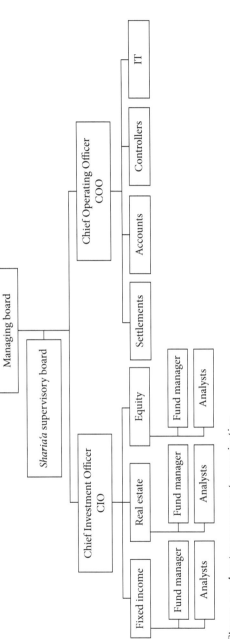

Figure 4.1 *Asset management organisation*

Sharia'a supervisory board is part of the structure. A more detailed description of the role of the *Sharia'a* supervisory board is included in Chapter 6.

Where a *Sharia'a*-compliant fund is part of a conventional bank or asset manager or an Islamic bank, the fund platform tends to have its own *Sharia'a* supervisory board. For a *Sharia'a*-compliant vehicle that is part of a conventional institution, the *Sharia'a* supervisory board is typically specifically appointed for the fund or fund platform. Where the fund is part of an Islamic financial institution, there are three options:

1. The fund's compliance is included in the overall *Sharia'a* compliance of the institution which is catered for by the institution's *Sharia'a* supervisory board.
2. The fund's compliance is segregated from the institution's but the fund's *Sharia'a* supervisory board consists of (a subset of) the same members as the parent company.
3. The fund's compliance is fully segregated from the institution and the fund appoints its own *Sharia'a* supervisory board.

4.2 Functions and roles

The organisation structure outlined in section 4.1 above identifies a variety of roles and responsibilities which are designed and structured in such a way as to ensure segregation of duties and appropriate corporate governance and to avoid conflicts of interest.

4.2.1 Managing board
The managing board acts as the supervisory board of the fund, and generally consists of a chairperson and two or

more members. It ultimately has overall responsibility for the running of the asset management company, or the asset management division of a bank, insurance company or institutional investor. The managing board defines and controls the strategic direction and although they can be appointed for a finite period of time, they are typically appointed for an indefinite period to ensure the asset management company or division is managed on a going-concern basis.

Different funds can be operated and managed by the same entity but each have their own strategic objectives. In addition, each of these funds may be incorporated in a different jurisdiction and have a variety of structures depending on the fund's requirements. Fund structures, for example, are generally set up to house multiple individual funds on the same platform which all come under the ultimate responsibility of the same general partner. Similar to conventional funds, *Sharia'a*-compliant funds can be structured as umbrella funds, open-ended investment companies (OEICs), collective investment schemes such as CIS and SICAV (*société d'investissement à capital variable*), undertakings for collective investments in transferable securities (UCITS) and any other generally accepted structure.

4.2.2 Sharia'a *supervisory board*

Although ultimate responsibility for *Sharia'a* compliance lies with the managing board, a *Sharia'a*-compliant fund will typically have a *Sharia'a* supervisory board consisting of at least one, but preferably two or three, *Sharia'a* scholars. The *Sharia'a* supervisory board is appointed at the incorporation of the fund, and ensures the transaction types as well as the general investment framework are both *Sharia'a* compliant. The role of the *Sharia'a* supervisory board is further defined in Chapter 6.

4.2.3 *Management functions*

The management functions of an asset manager consist of the chief investment officer and asset managers, whose respective roles are outlined below.

- **Chief investment officer.** The chief investment officer (CIO) oversees all investments and ensures that the investment restrictions are adhered to.
- **Asset manager.** Each fund is managed by a dedicated asset manager whose responsibility it is to ensure the monies are invested in the most efficient and effective way given the fund's investment mandate. Although asset managers typically manage more than one fund at a time, the funds they manage are generally in a similar area of the market. A typical fund management company is divided into the following areas:
  - fixed income, further subdivided into areas such as money markets, government bonds, credit and emerging markets
  - equity, which typically further houses private equity, public equity, venture capital and index funds; in addition, equities are typically broken up by region and size (large cap and small cap)
  - real estate, further subdivided into areas such as commercial property, private property and distressed property
  - alternative investments, under which would fall hedge funds, commodity funds and other alternative investment areas
  - multi-manager of fund or funds.

Although the above division is indicative, it provides an overview of the way funds are typically grouped into different areas. Individual asset management companies may, for example, only focus on one particular area or offer any combination of the above-listed areas and sub-areas.

Box 4.1 Analyst functions

Depending on the size of the fund, the asset class and available resources, both the nature and the depth of the analysis that is carried out may vary.

Equity
For equity-type funds, the focus of the analysis will typically lie on the opportunity to derive the fair value of the shares relative to the market and the peer group in which the asset can be placed. Within larger fund management operations, analysts typically specialise for example by geography (for example Asia, Europe, emerging markets), sector (for example institutional, technology, manufacturing) or market capitalisation (for example small cap versus large cap).

Fixed income
Analysts who operate in a fixed income environment generally also include credit analysis in their research.

Tools available
A large part of the work of an analyst involves the analysis of financial statements, industry analysis, review of economic circumstances and modelling.

Responsibilities
Where in large asset management firms the analyst generally has a specific, predefined role within the organisation, in smaller companies the analyst role is typically more varied and wider ranging; it is often also less detailed. Risk management may either be part of the analyst job or alternatively fall under the responsibility of a dedicated risk management department.

- **Analyst.** The role of the analyst differs per discipline and may cover a number of duties depending on the organisational structure. The main duty of an analyst is to analyse the securities that are held in a fund or those the fund intends to hold in the future. The nature of the analysis varies per type of fund, as outlined in Box 4.1.

4.2.4 Support functions

In order for funds to operate successfully, they need to rely on a large number of support functions to ensure that everything, including distribution, subscriptions and redemptions, transaction execution, and regulatory and general reporting, is executed smoothly. There are a number of generic support functions that can be identified and which are detailed below.

- **Distributor.** Distributors are third-party entities offering funds to investors and typically in a position to provide financial advice to retail and non-retail clients. Distributors include banks, brokerage firms and independent financial advisors. Many distributors offer platform solutions which enable investors to select from a range of investments without having to go to multiple distributors. Asset managers actively seek the distributors that provide them with the largest reach.
- **Accountant.** Funds are required to maintain their own set of accounts which includes balance sheet, profit and loss account, cash flow statements and a director's report. The accounts are audited by an independent external auditor. In addition, the accounts department independently verifies the fund's net asset value (NAV).
- **Administrator.** The fund administrator can be an

internal or external party and is independent from the fund manager. The administrators ensure subscriptions and associated funds are received and redemptions are paid out. The administrator handles investor inquiries and NAV reporting and ensures any other reporting requirements such as, for example, statistics and performance are met in a timely fashion. The administrator is further responsible for the management and execution of active transactions and payments, which includes account opening and closing, follow-up on corporate actions, reconciliation, tracking payments, valuation of securities for the NAV calculation and financial reporting. The administrator assigns and maintains ISINs (international securities identification number) and other codes to the funds they are responsible for.

- **Registrar.** The registrar is responsible for maintaining the register of owners of the shares in the fund. They register subscriptions and redemptions and ensure that contact details of the investors that are held on file are up to date at all times. In addition, the registrar ensures that the number of shares issued does not exceed the number authorised. A registrar is usually a bank or a trust company.

- **Transfer agent.** Similar to the registrar, the transfer agent maintains shareholder records including purchases, sales and account balances. In addition, the transfer agent matches the transactions from the asset managers and brokers.

- **Custodian.** The custodian is the entity that holds the invested assets on behalf of the fund and, by implication, the investors in the fund. It is typically an agent, bank or trust company.

- **Paying agent.** The responsibility of the paying agent is to ensure dividends, coupons and principal repayments on behalf of the issuer of the stocks or bonds. The paying agent of a fund is responsible for payments to investors on behalf of the fund.

- **External auditor.** The external auditor is responsible for independent verification of the fund's accounts, and will provide an opinion on whether or not they provide a true and fair view of the fund operations.
- **Legal advisor.** The legal advisor provides opinions on issues such as incorporation, tax, regulation and contract law. Depending on the structure of the fund, multiple legal advisors could be involved.

Each of these functions has to operate independently from the fund managers in order to ensure segregation of duties. In addition, most of the above-mentioned functions will provide their services to multiple funds, whether in-house or as an outsourced function. These funds do not necessarily have to be on the same platform or even managed by the same asset management company or asset management division of a bank. Some of the functions, such as accounting and internal audit, will generally be undertaken by an in-house department, whereas others are more likely to be performed by a third-party provider. Where the asset management division is part of a bank, functions such as the internal audit and paying agent can be performed by the audit and operations department of the bank respectively.

4.2.5 *Additional support functions: Index funds*
The support functions described in section 4.2.4 above are generic and although they are in some cases labelled differently, their general purpose is fairly consistent throughout.

In addition, some funds may require specific functions.

Index funds, for example, typically also involve index advisory and execution functions. Screening of eligible shares for *Sharia'a* compliance is typically done by specialist research companies which screen all individual constituents of the index to ensure they meet the criteria set out by the fund's *Sharia'a* supervisory board. With the availability of specialised *Sharia'a* indices such as the Dow Jones Islamic Market Index, the FTSE Shariah Global Index Series and the MSCI Islamic Index Series, most funds no longer construct their own index, but use one of these well-established indices as a benchmark. As detailed in section 3.6.1, constituents are screened on both their business activities and select financial ratios. Constituents that fail to pass either of these screens will be excluded from the index.

Although the above-mentioned indices are constructed to meet the individual criteria set out by the *Sharia'a* supervisory board and are generally based on the screening criteria outlined by AAOIFI, they may vary slightly.

The index advisory function reviews the different indices at the onset and recommends the most appropriate index to be used as a benchmark in line with the strategy of the fund. During the lifetime of the fund, the index advisory function reviews the continuing suitability of the index, and provides recommendations for any amendments to the index or its criteria.

The index execution function ensures that the investments the fund makes reflect the index as closely as possible. In order to fully match the benchmark the asset manager would have to be continuously invested in between 1,000 and 2,500 individual stock positions and will have to execute purchase and sale transactions on a continuous basis in order to exactly match the index. The transaction cost as well as the cost associated with monitoring in excess of 1,000 investments are prohibitive and have a severe impact on performance of the fund. In order to reduce transaction costs and still maintain performance levels similar to those of the index, the index execution team uses quantitative techniques which allow for the number of holdings and the number of transactions to be executed to be significantly lower.

4.3 Operations

Like any operations within a financial institution, functions need to be segregated to ensure that funds are processed efficiently and effectively with sufficient controls in place. Although different types of fund have slightly different specific requirements when it comes to the processing of individual transactions, the general operational requirements are the same for any fund. This section explores in detail the operational requirements regarding subscriptions, redemptions, NAV calculations, investment transactions and how investment decisions are made and carried out.

4.3.1 Reporting and disclosure

Funds are generally incorporated in international, tax-friendly jurisdictions. As a result they are regulated and need to meet the requirements of the regulator in the jurisdiction they are incorporated in, including particular reporting and disclosure requirements. Generally funds are required to produce and publish a balance sheet and profit and loss accounts at least annually. Although many funds opt to obtain a listing, this is not a requirement and not all funds do.

Generally investors tend to prefer regulated funds because they are subject to disclosure and reporting requirements thus providing investor comfort. Regulations differ per jurisdiction, but generally cover the following:

1. **Balance sheet.** The balance sheet reflects the state of the fund at the end of the reporting period and lists its assets, liabilities and capital and reserves.
2. **Profit and loss.** The profit and loss account reflects how the fund has fared over the current period and how it has distributed its profits.
3. **Additional information.** The additional information section may reflect anything the asset manager wishes to disclose about the fund itself such as performance over the period, asset allocations, top 10 holdings, an overview of the major risks, market commentary, concentrations and diversification.

4.4 Corporate governance

Similar to any other operation, corporate governance is an integral part of the set-up and can be deemed even more important for institutions that manage others' funds such as banks and other financial intermediaries. As the Organisation for Economic Co-operation and Development states (OECD 2004), the integrity of business and markets is vital to the financial stability of economies. As a result, good corporate governance is of the utmost importance. The OECD defines corporate governance as 'the rules and practices that govern the relationship between the managers and shareholders of corporations, as well as stakeholders like employees and creditors' (OECD 2004: 1).

The OECD Principles consist of 12 key standards covering six key areas of corporate governance. Combined, they contribute to growth and international financial stability and they form the basis for corporate governance systems. The principles defined in the six key areas aim to provide specific guidance for improvements to corporate governance frameworks and are aimed at policymakers,

Box 4.2 The OECD principles of corporate governance

1. **Ensuring the basis for an effective corporate governance framework.** The corporate governance framework should promote transparent and efficient markets, be consistent with the rule of law and clearly articulate the division of responsibilities among different supervisory, regulatory and enforcement authorities.

2. **The rights of shareholders and key ownership functions.** The corporate governance framework should protect and facilitate the exercise of shareholders' rights.

3. **The equitable treatment of shareholders.** The corporate governance framework should ensure the equitable treatment of all shareholders, including minority and foreign shareholders. All shareholders should have the opportunity to obtain effective redress for violation of their rights.

4. **The role of stakeholders in corporate governance.** The corporate governance framework should recognise the rights of stakeholders established by law or through mutual agreements and encourage active co-operation between corporations and stakeholders in creating wealth, jobs, and the sustainability of financially sound enterprises.

5. **Disclosure and transparency.** The corporate governance framework should ensure that timely and accurate disclosure is made on all material matters regarding the corporation, including the financial situation, performance, ownership, and governance of the company.

6. **The responsibilities of the board.** The corporate governance framework should ensure the strategic guidance of the company, the effective monitoring of management by the board, and the board's accountability to the company and the shareholders.

(OECD 2004)

regulators and market participants with a focus on publicly traded companies. The Financial Stability Forum has endorsed them as the key areas essential for financial stability. Originally issued in 1999, a revised version of the Principles was published in 2004. Since their inception, they have become the international benchmark for corporate governance.

Reviewing the main areas of the OECD principles for corporate governance in a bit more detail shows clearly that most, if not all, of these principles are naturally in line with the ethical principles underpinning *Sharia'a*, particularly those dealing with how to conduct business. A particularly close link can be found in the annotations to the principles (OECD 2004a: 30), which stress that 'corporate governance frameworks should be developed with a view to its impact on overall economic performance, market integrity and the incentives it creates for market participants and the promotion of transparent and efficient markets.'

Effective corporate governance typically incorporates the following elements:

- **Board structure.** The board structure should be such that there is sufficient segregation of duties, and a concentration of too much power in one hand is avoided. Examples of issues that need to be considered are the level of independence and number of non-executive directors, as well as the desirability of segregating the chair function from the chief executive officer function. The balance between the number of executive and non-executive directors on the board is of importance in order to ensure independence of the board. After all, a significantly higher number of executive directors may create the impression that the independence of the board is potentially jeopardised. In addition, board committees such as the audit committee, the nominations committee and remuneration committee are designed to advise the board independently from the CEO and the other executive directors. The board typically meets once per quarter, unless additional meetings are required. Outside the scheduled meetings, additional meetings can be called by the chair of the board.

- **Annual report.** The annual report provides the owners of the company (the shareholders) with information about the financial position of the company, how it has performed and how its cash has been generated. The underlying documentation such as balance sheet and profit and loss accounts can be used by the board of directors as grounds for discharging the CEO and executive directors of their duties.

- **Independent external auditors.** The role of the independent auditor is to ensure that the annual report provides a true and fair view of the company's activities, independently of the CEO and directors.

- **Annual general meeting.** The annual general meeting (AGM) or shareholders' meeting allows the shareholders to put questions to the directors and they have the right to appoint and remove directors and external auditors. The shareholders' meeting is typically held once a year after the annual report has been published.

- **Insolvency procedures.** These procedures outline how, in case of the inability of the corporation to pay its creditors, certain rights of governance pass to creditors' representatives in order to minimise their losses. The basic purpose of insolvency procedures is to provide a certain level of protection to lenders and creditors.

Sharia'a-compliant financial institutions have an additional organ of governance in the *Sharia'a* supervisory board, which is incorporated to independently ensure that the activities of the corporation are compliant with *Sharia'a*. The *Sharia'a* supervisory board generally consists of between three and five part-time members and its role is described in detail in Chapter 6.

4.4.1 Compliance requirements

In order to prevent a fund or fund management company from being used for potential money laundering or other forms of financial crime, as well as to prevent potential reputational risk associated with, for instance, clients or marketing materials, the fund is subject to the same rigorous compliance requirements that are prescribed by the regulators of the jurisdiction where the fund management company or the bank is incorporated. The requirements differ per location and are in part dependent on the maturity of the local market. However, many funds seek authorisation and listing in international financial markets and will as a result have to follow their regulatory regime which includes compliance requirements. The remainder of this section is based on the requirements specified by the Financial Services Authority (FSA) in the United Kingdom and can be taken to represent the standard for all Western regulators. One of the main general requirements for authorised firms is that they:

> must have robust governance arrangements including a clear organisational structure and well defined, transparent and consistent lines of responsibility, effective processes to identify, manage, monitor and report the risks it is or might be exposed to, and internal control mechanisms, including sound administrative and accounting procedures and effective control and safeguard arrangements for information processing systems.[1]

It is important to bear in mind that final responsibility for the firm lies with senior management and cannot be delegated. One of the measures to safeguard this is to ensure that individuals holding senior management positions within a firm have a sufficiently good reputation and have the right level of knowledge and experience. Segregation of duties, the introduction of Chinese walls and client assessment procedures further enhance the efficiency and effectiveness of the firm and its appropriate working within the financial industry.

The compliance function plays an important role in ensuring that the firm's actions are aligned with the principles of good governance, that there are no criminal or adverse dealings and that the firm acts in the best interest of its clients. The main policies for compliance are associated with the following issues:

- **Conflict of interest.** There are a number of ways in which conflicts of interest can occur, and they can generally be defined as a situation in which an individual or the firm is involved in multiple interests that may not be aligned. For example, an analyst with a large shareholding is more likely to make a buy recommendation for the same shares than a sell or hold recommendation. His own shareholding has resulted in a biased opinion. Any potential conflicts of interest need to be reported and dealt with on a case-by-case basis to ensure they don't have an adverse impact on either the firm, the employee or the client. The severity of the controls put in place will depend on the individual situation. On the one hand it might, for example, be sufficient to declare a shareholding when making a recommendation to buy or sell to a client. On the other hand, there may be situations where it would be more appropriate to remove an employee from a particular account to avoid any suspicion.

- **Know your customer (KYC).** Financial firms need to employ a due diligence process to identify their clients and to obtain any relevant information to verify their identity. KYC is an important process in the prevention of money laundering and terrorist financing, but is also used to ensure the firm does not run any reputational risk from being involved in transactions with people or organisations engaged in these activities. As part of the KYC process, the firm typically also takes a view on any politically exposed persons, and those who may have been associated with fraud or other potentially damaging publicity. As part of the KYC process, the institution will carry out a customer assessment to determine the risk profile of the client and suitability of instruments.

- **Customer assessment.** In the majority of international jurisdictions it is the responsibility of a financial firm to ensure a sufficient level of customer protection, in particular for those customer groups that are vulnerable, such as small retail clients. Customer assessment is generally part of the KYC process, but will only be executed once the institution has decided to enter into a relationship with the client. It is the responsibility of the firm to ensure that clients are aware of the financial risks they take and are protected from any unnecessary risk. The Markets in Financial Investments Directive (MiFID) provides European-wide legislation regarding customer categorisation and identifies three types of counterparty, each with different levels of protection, as detailed below.[2] It needs to be considered that these are European-wide regulations and although quite generic, implementation may differ in individual European jurisdictions as well as outside of the European Economic Area (EEA).

1. **Retail client.** This is the least sophisticated type of client and covers any client which does not fall into the other two categories. It is also the client category that, due to its lack of sophistication and understanding of financial transactions, requires the highest level of protection.

2. **Professional client.** These are clients that routinely carry out financial transactions and include institutions authorised and regulated in the EEA such as credit unions, investment firms and institutional investors. In addition, other large undertakings such as companies, partnerships or trusts may qualify as professional clients as long as they meet the size requirements for the balance sheet, turnover or number of members. A retail client can be upgraded to a professional client as long as the client has proven experience with financial instruments, the client's investments exceed €500,000 and the client has stated in writing that they wish to be classified as a professional client, confirming they understand the additional risks associated with losing retail client protections.

3. **Eligible counterparty.** These are deemed to be the most sophisticated counterparties that have the least protection. Insurance companies, funds, investment firms, central banks and financial institutions authorised and regulated by regulators either within or outside the EEA are among the types of institution that are automatically classified as eligible counterparties. In addition, corporates can be elected to be eligible counterparties if they fulfil a set number of criteria defined in the MiFID regulations.

- **Chinese wall.** Chinese walls are virtual arrangements

that are put in place to ensure that information that is held in one part of the organisation is withheld from other parts of the organisation. Information may need to be privileged for different reasons such as sensitivity of information in the market or to avoid potential conflicts of interest.

- **Financial crime.** Financial crime encompasses money laundering, tax evasion and fraud and is a risk that needs to be monitored carefully. Anti-money-laundering regulations are generally embedded in both criminal law (such as the Serious Organised Crime Act in the United Kingdom and the Financial Crimes Enforcement Network in the United States) as well as in financial regulations. This is similarly the case for counter-terrorist financing and fraud regulations.

- **Financial promotions.** The financial institution has to ensure that any promotional material they produce is true, fair and not misleading. This implies for example that the firm cannot make any statements regarding profitability of an investment without drawing attention to the potential risks involved and without appropriate underlying evidence.

Although the above are not exhaustive, they provide a good overview of the compliance requirements a financial firm needs to fulfil. These requirements apply to a wide range of financial firms including (Islamic) asset management firms.

Sharia'a compliance

As an additional requirement, Islamic financial institutions have to ensure that all their transactions and operations are *Sharia'a* compliant. Where Islamic financial services are offered by a conventional firm, it is the firm's responsibility to ensure that the conventional and Islamic financial services operate with segregated operations and accounts. Although the ultimate responsibility for *Sharia'a* compliance lies with the senior management of the institution, the day-to-day responsibility can for example be delegated to the legal department, compliance or a specialised *Sharia'a* compliance function. More detail on *Sharia'a* compliance and the role of the *Sharia'a* supervisory board can be found in Chapter 6.

Notes

1. *FSA Handbook, Systems and Controls* (June 2010), http://fsahandbook.info/fsa//handbook/sysc.pdf, section 4.1, rule 4.1.1.
2. It is beyond the scope of this book to provide a full overview of the MiFID regulations. However, a full description of the rules can be found on the website of the European Union, at http://ec.europa.eu/internal_market/securities/isd/index_en.htm

CHAPTER 5
PROCESSING

Similar to conventional funds, Islamic funds have to manage a number of processes, including subscriptions and redemptions, investments, accounting and reporting, payment processing, and risk and liquidity management. Each of these processes is outlined in more detail in this section. However, it needs to be considered that these descriptions are generic and high-level only. Individual funds may apply different criteria and processes.

5.1 Prior to incorporation

Prior to the incorporation of the fund, the structure, location of incorporation and third-party service providers need to be decided upon. The legal jurisdiction is normally chosen in such a way that it provides optimum tax efficiency given the target client base, and is in addition generally a jurisdiction with a solid regulatory environment. The choice of jurisdiction of incorporation impacts a number of areas including tax treatment, listing requirements, regulatory reporting and any other associated issues.

5.1.1 *Fund structure*

The mutual fund or collective investment scheme structure appears to be prevalent for many types of fund including Islamic fund structures. Funds are often structured as open-ended investment companies (OEIC), unit trusts (UT) or investment trusts (IT), although other, similar, structures such as the European OIEC equivalent *société d'investissement à capital variable* (SICAV) are equally applied.

Third-party service providers such as investment advisors, distributors, independent accountants, administrators and custodians are, where applicable, appointed as early as possible in the process of setting up a new fund. The *Sharia'a* supervisory board is generally appointed prior to incorporation of the fund, and is actively involved in the determination of the guidelines and parameters of the fund in order to ensure the fund is set up to be a *Sharia'a*-compliant vehicle from the outset.

Once the fund structure is defined and the parameters of investment are decided upon, the asset management company or division produces the information or offering memorandum which outlines the details of the fund including investment objective, applicable charges, any conditions and legal and regulatory requirements. It is worth bearing in mind that any cost associated with subscriptions, transfers, switching and redemptions are included in the conditions.

5.1.2 *Investment mandate*

As part of the structure, the fund's board determines the investment mandate which provides the framework for the fund manager's investment decisions. The investment mandate generally includes the following criteria:

- **Objective.** A fund's objective is typically to achieve the best possible return relative to an applicable benchmark and within the constraints outlined in the investment mandate.
- **General constraints.** The fund's general constraints identify how excess returns can be achieved, the type of exposure the fund is willing to take and the risk appetite of the fund. General constraints may, for example, be used to define how active risk positions are managed, whether the investment strategy is active or passive, how close the fund's yield is supposed to be to the benchmark, and the risk parameters within which the fund may be managed. Some examples of general constraints are outlined in Box 5.1. The examples show that the general constraints are very high level and although they set the accepted framework for the fund itself, they still need to be fine tuned further. The general constraints for a *Sharia'a*-compliant fund will in addition have a reference to the fact that all investments and assets must be *Sharia'a* compliant.
- **Investment universe.** The fund's investment universe identifies the constraints within which all investments need to be made. The constraints include the relevant laws and regulations as well as any other restrictions the fund owner, the fund's board of directors and the fund's *Sharia'a* supervisory board deem suitable given the risk appetite of the fund and the type of investment suitable for the type of fund. For example, for a *Sharia'a*-compliant money market fund the investment universe could be restricted to *sukuk*, *wakala*, commodity *murabaha* and other interest-free deposits. The constraints surrounding *Sharia'a* compliance of the instruments will be part of the specifications of the investment universe.
- **Investment restrictions.** Further restrictions can be

Box 5.1 General constraints

Example 1: Norges Bank Investment Management
Norges Bank Investment Management (NBIM) defines its
general constraints as follows:[1]

Excess return on the portfolio shall be achieved in a control-
led manner and with limited systematic exposure to priced
risk factors in the markets. The portfolio shall be managed
in accordance with the Executive Boards Principles for risk
management in NBIM.

Active risk positions are to be taken in a balanced manner
such that no single position accounts for a high portion of total
risk exposure. Active investment strategies with significantly
skewed outcomes (tail risk) shall be monitored and reported
separately. The yield to maturity in the fixed income portfolio
must not systematically be markedly higher than the yield in
the benchmark portfolio. The portfolio shall be managed in
such a way that the active positions can be reduced to provide
liquidity for expected and unexpected changes in the composi-
tion of the benchmark portfolio without incurring abnormally
high transaction costs.

The portfolio shall be rebalanced in accordance with the
applicable guidelines for rebalancing.

Example 2: Durban Pension Fund
The Durban Pension Fund has a different set of constraints
that need to be complied with unless otherwise approved by
the trustees. They are defined as follows:[2]

No more than 7.5% of the Fund's assets may be invested in
a single holding with the exception of Government bonds
provided that where specifically motivated by an investment
manager the Investment Sub-Committee has been delegated
authority to permit investment up to 15%.

An equity holding in any particular company (or companies

---

in a related pyramid structure) may not exceed 2.5% of the total market capitalisation of that company (or the base company in a pyramid Investment Policy Document structure) if the company or base company's market capitalisation is less than R3 billion.

An equity holding in any particular company (or companies in a related pyramid structure) may not exceed 5% of the total market capitalisation of that company (or the base company in a pyramid structure) if the company or base company's market capitalisation exceeds R3 billion.

General constraints in a Sharia'a-compliant fund

The general constraints for a *Sharia'a*-compliant fund are typically highly similar to any general constraints defined for conventional funds. However, they will in addition refer to the fact that all underlying investments, liquidity instruments and other assets will need to be *Sharia'a* compliant.

Example 3: Al Rajhi Global Small Cap Equity Fund

Al Rajhi Global Small Cap Equity Fund is a *Sharia'a*-compliant fund which identifies its investment strategy as follows:[3]

- The fund invests predominantly in *Sharia'a*-compliant equities of small-sized companies listed and traded on major stock exchanges across the world with a long-term horizon.
- The asset allocation is determined by general market conditions with well-diversified sector allocation. The fund selects stocks with good management and small capital. They have greater potential of success and manifest higher growth with rapid appreciation in their market values.
- The investment would primarily be focused mostly in the USA and could be diversified into Western Europe and other Asian countries.
- The fund is optimised by using sophisticated investment techniques by maximising returns and minimising risk while measuring the performance against the benchmark index.

put in place which reflect the risk appetite of the fund. These restrictions could for example specify any deviations from a benchmark portfolio or *Sharia'a*-compliant index or specify the maximum allocation to a geographical region, asset class or sector deviation. For example, a *Sharia'a*-compliant money market fund could specify a maximum of 60 per cent invested in *sukuk*, with a minimum credit rating of BBB, a maximum investment in a particular geographical region of 30 per cent and unrestricted investment in government securities. Restrictions are generally put in place to ensure the investments in the fund match its risk appetite, and could include the assignment of voting rights.

- **Counterparty restrictions.** In addition to restrictions on the investments and their risk, further restrictions can be placed on the creditworthiness of the counterparties to restrict counterparty credit risk. This restriction is particularly relevant when placing *Sharia'a*-compliant deposits with a counterparty. A counterparty restriction could, for example, be that deposits on a *wakala* basis can only be placed with fully *Sharia'a*-compliant financial institutions with a rating of BBB or above and that for all other counterparties a commodity *murabaha* transaction is to be applied. Netting agreements and potential future counterparty exposure levels could be part of the restrictions.
- **Delegation.** The investment mandate may specify that third party fund managers may be appointed for particular segments of the fund, sub-funds or portfolios. In the event management is delegated, segregate investment mandates need to be provided to each compartment in line with the overall investment strategy.
- **Reporting.** Any particular reporting including, but not

restricted to, accounts, risk reporting, exception reporting and reporting requirements for the *Sharia'a* supervisory board need to be specified in the investment mandate including their frequency, audience and level of detail.

5.1.3 Applicable benchmark

The performance of a fund is usually measured against a suitable benchmark, for example an internationally established index like the FTSE 100, or Dow Jones Emerging Markets. The benchmark needs to be chosen in such a way that it is realistically achievable and reflects the fund objectives and constraints.

Historically, the performance of Islamic funds has long been measured against conventional benchmarks such as the FTSE Emerging Markets Index or MSCI Worldscope. The disadvantage of this is immediately obvious since the benchmarks do not reflect the principles underlying *Sharia'a* as they are constituted without any of these considerations in mind. Certain components that make up a large part of a conventional index such as Financial Institutions are prohibited as an investment for *Sharia'a*-compliant funds and adjustments will need to be made to cater for these differences. In addition, adjustments will have to be made to cater for other non-compliant income. Since late 1998, however, *Sharia'a*-compliant indices have started to become available which exclude any non-*Sharia'a*-compliant investments on the basis of business activity and financial ratios. These indices provide a more accurate benchmark and are described in detail in section 3.6.5.

5.2 Subscriptions, redemptions, switches and transfers

Subscriptions, switches, transfers and redemptions are the activities associated with the processing of client monies, each of which is described in this section. Any costs and charges associated with these elements are outlined in the information or offering memorandum and may be summarised in any material that is produced as part of the fund's marketing material.

5.2.1 *Subscriptions*

Subscriptions to a fund are the amounts received from clients for investment. Prior to accepting the funds, the firm needs to ensure that all KYC procedures have been duly followed, including an assessment of suitability of the client for purposes of the fund. The subscription process is depicted in Figure 5.1.

Once a subscription form is received, the back office checks whether the client is new or existing and, if necessary, ensures the KYC process as defined in section 4.4.1 is undertaken. As part of the KYC process, the suitability of the fund for the client is also assessed. Some funds are, for example, restricted to eligible counterparties only.

Upon successful completion of the KYC and assessment processes, the back office initiates the process of accepting client monies and investing the same into the fund. The back office informs the fund administrator, who will monitor the receipt of the monies, and sends a confirmation to the client stating the amount received, the price at which the units are bought (typically the current NAV), the class of shares and the number of units.

The funds are subsequently released to the fund manager for investment purposes.

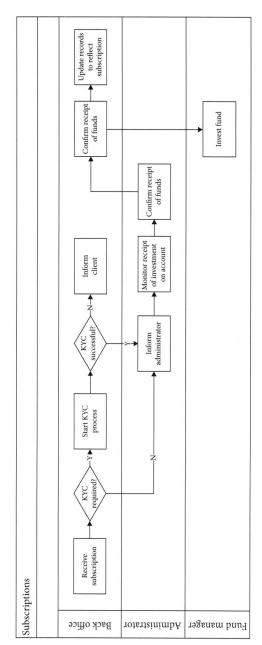

Figure 5.1 *Subscriptions*

5.2.2 *Switches and transfers*

Switches and transfers occur when investors retain their funds with the same asset management company or even on the same fund platform within that. In switches, the clients change their investment from one fund to another one. In transfers, the client requests a transfer of ownership for their units. Switches and transfers occur for a variety of reasons, for example diversification, tax efficiency and changes in investment horizon and risk appetite.

Fund switches

A fund switch occurs when an investor switches a number of units or shares in a particular fund for another investment in the same range of funds, and is historically associated with mutual funds although the practice has spread to other funds as well. The rationale for fund switching is generally to achieve higher returns, and is typically done as economic climates and market trends change. The next big reason for fund switching is a change in investor risk profile, preference and investment horizon resulting in a rebalancing of the portfolio.

The switching process can be broken down into the following steps:

1. **Sale of units of shares.** This step consists of the sale of the required number of units of shares in the fund the investor is currently invested in. For dual priced units, the sale normally takes place at the bid price which is usually at a discount to the NAV to reflect any administrative charges. If the investor is required to pay capital gains tax in his country of domicile, the sale of shares is typically treated as a disposal for this purpose which implies the investor may have to pay capital gains tax if the sale is made at a profit. OEIC and SICAV struc-

tures, which have gained a dominant position in the market, are single priced, which implies that there is only one NAV quoted for the unit, which is used for both subscriptions and redemptions.

2. **Purchase of units or shares.** The second step in the process uses the proceeds from step 1 to purchase units in the alternative fund selected. The purchase takes place at the offer price, which is typically NAV plus administrative charges, or the mid-price in the event of a single priced OEIC or SICAV.

In a *Sharia'a*-compliant fund, the administrative charges should not be in proportion to the funds invested or withdrawn, but should solely reflect the actual cost associated with the switching process. Typically the fund manager would not charge any additional cost for switching, since the funds are retained by the company even though they are no longer invested in the same fund. The asset manager may chose to restrict the allowable number of switches per annum and can apply a fee in the event this threshold is exceeded. Thresholds are typically introduced to protect shareholders from unnecessary charges arising from the churning of assets in the fund.

Fund transfers
Transfers occur in the event ownership of the units in a fund is transferred from one person to another. There are various circumstances in which this could be allowed, for example a transfer of units from parents to their children when the children reach their eighteenth birthday. From the fund manager's perspective the transaction is only a change of ownership in the register, and there is typically no charge associated with the transaction although the number of transfers and the parties that transfers can be made to

may contractually be limited. The original unit holders can transfer part or all or their existing holdings to the new owners.

5.2.3 Redemptions

Redemptions refer to the process of refunding an investor for returning part or all their units in the fund and can occur either at the end date of the fund or before. Redemptions can be subject to criteria such as minimum and maximum redemption amounts, minimum subscription periods prior to which no redemptions are allowed, notice periods and, in some cases, exit fees.

Criteria regarding maximum redemption amounts are commonly known as gates and are for example expressed as a percentage of net fund assets. Gates are a common feature with illiquid funds and provide a liquidity management tool for fund managers.

Minimum subscription periods are generally put in place to ensure the fund manager can recoup some of the transaction cost associated with the initial investments and spread them out over time. These costs are part of the general operating costs of the fund. When such costs are deemed excessive, the fund manager has the discretion to apply a dilution levy or swing pricing. Both these measures are to protect existing shareholders from excessive costs caused by a small number of investors. The ability of the fund manager to apply these charges is defined in the offering memorandum or prospectus of the fund.

In addition to the above, redemption can be subject to fixed schedules or notice periods. Many hedge funds for example operate an end-of-quarter redemption policy with a 90-day notice period. This implies that in order to be repaid at the end of a particular quarter, the investor will have to notify the fund around the end of the quarter prior to the desired redemption date. The redemption process is shown in Figure 5.2.

Once the redemption request is received it is checked by the back office in order to ensure the request meets the general redemption criteria specified in the fund documentation and that the amount or number of units requested to be redeemed is not in excess of the investor's holding in the fund. Units can be redeemed against the most recent NAV, less any pre-notified redemption cost. More generally, particularly for mutual funds, units are redeemed on a forward pricing basis, which means that units are redeemed on the next NAV date using the NAV on that date.

5.3 Investment process

Once funds are received into the fund, the fund manager will deploy them in line with the general fund parameters. The fund manager is continuously trying to identify those investments that will provide a higher return, for example by taking a higher risk, making use of a temporary shift in investor opinion, or by identifying stocks for which the fund manager expects a higher dividend than the market. The fund manager makes investment decisions bearing in mind the following:

- **Type of fund.** Whether a fund is a money market-type fund, real estate, private equity or takes any other form strongly dictates the initial parameters the fund manager needs to work within, and the type of investment the fund manager is restricted to for inclusion in the fund.
- **Desired risk level.** The fund's risk appetite is typically defined as part of the general parameters albeit in fairly generic terms. Although some funds have a capital

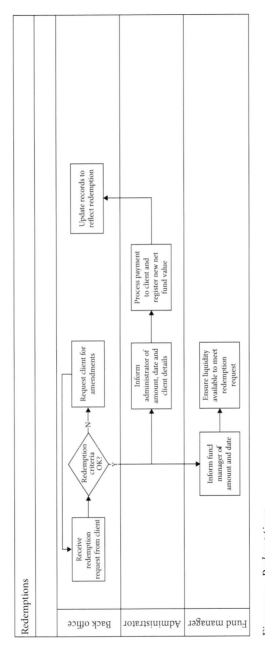

Figure 5.2 *Redemptions*

protection, the majority of funds will define risk levels along the lines of low, medium and high. Any investment proposed by the fund manager will be reviewed against these criteria and included if it is deemed suitable.

- **Diversification.** Within the parameters of the fund, which may for example dictate a focus on a particular geography, sector, size or instrument types, the fund manager may rebalance the fund, or purchase or sell particular investments in order to ensure that the fund is suitably diversified and not subject to concentration risk.

- **Relative maturity.** Funds are typically managed to have a time horizon that matches the type of fund and risk levels. Any investment will need to be judged against this requirement. In addition, substitution investments may be considered, for example by selling a bond with a short maturity and purchasing a bond with similar characteristics, issued by the same issuer with a longer-dated maturity.

- **Liquidity requirements.** As part of the investment decision-making process, the fund manager is required to balance the funds under management between different liquidity classes. Liquidity has an impact on performance in such a way that highly liquid instruments such as cash or short-term deposits are typically providing lower returns than other instruments with a more illiquid nature.

- **Total size of the invested asset.** In particular for non-real estate funds, fund managers tend to avoid being the sole investor in any single asset. There are different considerations depending on the type of fund, some of which are as follows:

  1. **Private equity.** Generally, the private equity fund manager would require the owner of the business to

also retain a level of investment in the fund. Private equity investments are generally subject to lock-in periods and redemption notice periods.

2. **Money market instruments.** Typically both a minimum investment amount per instrument and a minimum issue size requirement are applied. Many fund managers would for example not invest in any money market instrument for which the issue size is below $100 million. Additional criteria such as a minimum investment amount are often combined with a percentage of the total issue. For example, minimum investment $10 million, and not more than 10 per cent of the total amount in issue.

3. **Fund of funds.** Fund of fund managers tend to work with minimum investment amounts in combination with a maximum percentage of funds under management. Fund of funds generally involve additional fees charged by the fund of funds manager which are charged in addition to the fees payable to the underlying funds.

Once an investment is made, it is monitored on an ongoing basis to ensure that it still fits within the overall strategy of the fund. For *Sharia'a*-compliant funds, the investments are also monitored so as to ensure ongoing *Sharia'a* compliance, the monitoring of which as well as the actions to be taken in the event of non-compliance are further described in Chapter 6.

The investment process is relatively straightforward, as outlined in Figure 5.3. The fund manager reviews the initial opportunity to invest which may be brought to his attention by different sources such as the analyst, a road show or a news item. Typically, the analyst then provides further research and may present the instrument or transaction structure

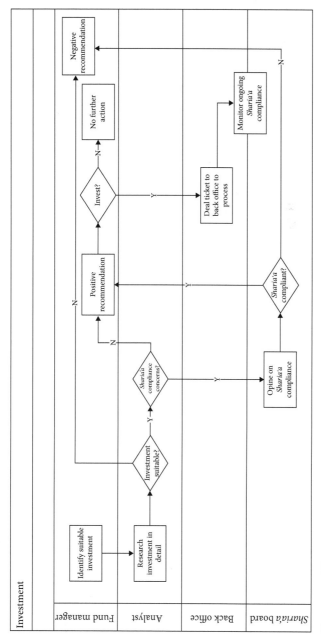

Figure 5.3 *The investment process*

to the *Sharia'a* supervisory board in the event there are any concerns regarding the acceptability of the transactions. Generally, if the analyst has significant concerns about the compliance of a transaction this would in any case result in a negative recommendation, and only instruments where there are minor concerns will be presented to the *Sharia'a* supervisory board. Formal verification of new instruments and issues will in any case be required. Once the analyst has finalised the research, they will provide a recommendation to the fund manager, who will then make the final investment decision. An investment committee generally formalises this process. In the event the fund manager decides to invest, they will execute a transaction in the market and provide the transaction details to the back office in the form of a deal ticket. The back office will then process the transaction and associated payments to fully settle the trade. This includes informing the custodian, in its capacity as the keeper of the assets on behalf of the investors, of the amount and type of investments to be received.

Once an instrument or particular investment is included in the fund, *Sharia'a* compliance is monitored on an ongoing basis. In the event non-compliance occurs, disinvestment may need to take place. For further information about this process, see Chapter 6.

5.4 Payments and receipts

Depending on the type of fund, there is a variety of payments and receipts as part of the fund operations. Depending on the type of fund, the receipts into a fund could, for instance, consist of any of the following:

- subscriptions
- sale proceeds of *sukuk*, leases or other instruments

- periodic coupons
- periodic rentals
- reimbursement of *wakala*-invested amounts plus a profit share (if any)
- repayment of commodity *murabaha* plus mark-up
- repayment of *sukuk* principal amount at maturity.

Typically any cash paid into the fund is held by the custodian in a segregated bank account opened in the name of the fund's legal entity. Amounts in a foreign currency may be held at correspondent banks or financial institutions, although these will again have to be in the name of the fund's legal entity.

In turn, the custodian is responsible to make or effect payments, upon receipt of the appropriate instructions from the authorised officers of the fund, to meet the fund's obligations as they arise from time to time. Payments include, but are not restricted to, any of the following:

- tax payments
- administration fees
- custodian fees
- payments to satisfy the obligations arising from a *sukuk* purchase
- payments for leased assets
- legal fees
- *wakala* deposits
- commodity *murabaha* payments associated with the purchase of the assets
- redemptions to investors
- payments of charitable donations for the purification of the proportion of dividends associated with non-compliant investment income (in particular for equity-type investments).

All payments and receipts need to be verified independently against the appropriate documentation and reconciled against the expected payments and receipts. When the client wishes to sell a specific number of units, redemption payments need to be determined at the number of units redeemed multiplied by the NAV per unit. For more traditional consideration-based transactions, the number of units to be redeemed will be derived from the total consideration required and the NAV applicable at the time of redemption.

5.5 Settlement, accounting and reporting

Generally speaking, funds tend to have a two-tier accounting structure. The administration function maintains the books and records of all funds on the same platform and arranges for the calculation of the NAV per unit of investment. Where this function is outsourced, which may for example occur for smaller companies, a fund has its own internal accountant who will independently verify and agree the NAV, and who is responsible for the day-to-day due diligence and accounting activities such as the production of a statement of profit and loss to monitor the activities undertaken by the outsourced administrator.

The administrator's role can be broken down into a number of main parts with regard to accounting and reporting.

5.5.1 *Reconciliation, verification and accounting*
The administrator collects confirmations from different parties and executes an independent reconciliation to ensure all information is in order. If any discrepancies or anomalies occur, the administrator contacts the relevant parties to resolve the issue. Once resolved, a new confirmation will be submitted and a final verification will take place.

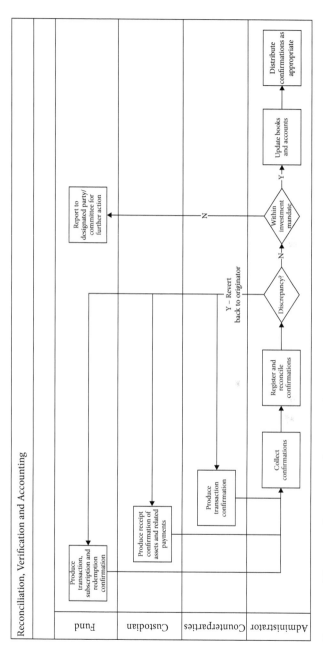

Reconciliation, Verification and Accounting

	Fund	Custodian	Counterparties	Administrator

Fund: Produce transaction, subscription and redemption confirmation

Custodian: Produce receipt confirmation of assets and related payments

Counterparties: Produce transaction confirmation

Administrator: Collect confirmations → Register and reconcile confirmations → Discrepancy?

Discrepancy? — Y – Revert back to originator

Discrepancy? — N → Within investment mandate?

Within investment mandate? — N → Report to designated party/committee for further action

Within investment mandate? — Y → Update books and accounts → Distribute confirmations as appropriate

Figure 5.4   *The reconciliation, verification and accounting process*

The administrator will then proceed to verify whether the transaction is within the restrictions specified in the investment mandate. It is outside the remit of the administrator to take any corrective actions: the administrator's role ends with reporting any breach to the relevant parties such as the fund's board of directors or auditors. Once all is verified and in order, the administrator updates the books and accounts and distributes the relevant information as appropriate. The administrator maintains an independent set of accounts from the fund accountant.

5.5.2 *Reporting and record keeping*

On a periodic basis, the administrator produces and publishes the financial reports including a balance sheet and profit and loss accounts as well as any other statements required under the laws and regulations applicable to the jurisdiction of incorporation and as laid down in the fund set up. The administrator provides this and other required information to the fund manager, the fund accountant and the custodian. It is the administrator's responsibility to ensure annual, semi-annual, monthly and other statements are filed with the regulatory authorities. The administrator maintains all records safely for the required period of time in line with the requirements of the local laws and regulations and the fund's requirements.

5.5.3 *Recording of shareholder details, payments and receipts*

All applications for subscriptions, redemptions, conversions and share transfers are received by the administrator and details of the shareholder are duly registered. The administrator is responsible for the verification of the investor identity in relation to any of these requests. Any know-your-customer procedures can either be executed by the administrator or a compliance function associated with the fund. The administrator verifies the amounts received from investors against the transaction instructions and ensures the fund manager is informed accordingly. Any payments of dividends and redemptions are executed by the administrator. Once the transaction and shareholder details are verified payments are made to the account details pecified in the shareholder register.

5.6 Net asset value calculation

Periodically the administrator determines the value of the assets held in each of the different funds and fund compartments under its responsibility. The methodology applied to determine the value of the assets is part of the fund's structure and is typically communicated to the investors via the offering memorandum or any other official form of communication thereafter.

5.6.1 Periodicity

The periodicity with which the value of each asset is determined is directly related to the periodicity of the publication of the net asset value (NAV) and is determined as part of the fund structure. Although many conventional funds publish daily NAVs, *Sharia'a*-compliant funds tend to publish their NAVs less frequently. *Sharia'a*-compliant funds have predominantly published their NAVs on a monthly basis. However, there appears to be a trend towards changing this to weekly and, occasionally, even more frequently. Particularly for money market- and leasing-type funds, daily and weekly publication would make the funds more attractive to a wider range of investors and would also attract investors that are not necessarily looking for *Sharia'a* compliance, but have an interest in the underlying principles.

5.6.2 *Calculation*

The exact calculation of the value of any asset is outlined in the valuation methodology defined in the fund strategy and will largely depend on the type of asset in combination with its liquidity in the market and accounting treatment requirements. There are a variety of valuation methodologies that can be applied, the main ones being straight line, fair value and historical cost. A discussion of when to apply each of these methods is outside the remit of this book, but some of the potential challenges for *Sharia'a*-compliant funds are outlined below.

Fair value

Fair value accounting is generally speaking applied to assets that are held with the intention to sell, although this does not imply they have to be sold prior to maturity. Under fair value accounting rules, the value of an asset is determined based on either observable prices in the market for the same asset (mark to market) or by using a model that applies observable inputs such as quoted prices for comparable assets and other relevant market data. This is sometimes referred to as mark to model, and is typically used when prices in the market are erratic, sparse or generally unobtainable. The types of asset that can be held by *Sharia'a*-compliant funds that would qualify for the fair value treatment are investments in public and private equity, *sukuk* and, in some cases, real estate investments although particularly the latter are generally considered to be too illiquid and the valuation may not provide a realistic sale value.

- **Public equity** can easily be valued on a daily basis by using the closing prices observed on the stock exchange where the stock is listed.
- **Private equity** is more difficult due to the fact that there

are no prices available in the market. Prices for comparable companies and other market factors such as the development of the industry and cash flow and residual income valuation techniques can be applied to obtain a reasonable current value.

- *Sukuk* valuation differs per issue depending on listing and availability of quoted prices. Many *sukuk* are held to maturity and prone to unrelated news, as the announcement of the Dubai World debt restructure in November 2009 has clearly shown (see also box 5.2). Prices are not always available and, when available, often differ widely.

- **Real estate** is generally valued at historical cost minus any impairments although regular valuations will be obtained. The real estate investment market, particularly when it concerns commercial real estate, is fairly illiquid and any valuation is not necessarily a reflection of the price that can be realised in the open market.

Straight line
For assets where market prices are difficult to obtain, a straight line valuation can be applied, which implies adding the daily amortisation of the expected repayment on the next payment date to the original investment. Straight line valuation can be used for example to value lease investments or *sukuk,* as long as the investment has a periodic payment associated with it.

Historical cost minus impairments
Assets held to maturity as well as assets for which market values cannot be obtained are generally valued at original purchase cost minus any impairments. Historical costs are generally perceived to be the fair value at the time the asset was purchased.

Box 5.2 Fair value valuation: *sukuk* valuation

Sukuk currently in issue is generally short dated with an average maturity of up to five years and has historically been more generously priced than conventional bond issues with comparable characteristics. *Sukuk* is more in line with *Sharia'a* compliance than alternative short-term investments such as commodity *murabaha,* and many Islamic financial institutions have started purchasing *sukuk*, choosing to hold it to maturity. In addition, the short maturities in combination with the higher than average pricing has made *sukuk* an attractive investment opportunity for conventional financial institutions. The majority of *sukuk* is bought in the primary market, and the secondary market is still relatively under-developed, which has a notable impact on the pricing in the secondary market. As can be seen from Figure 5.5 which charts the average market price quoted for 12 randomly selected *sukuk* issues, all issued by corporates in the Middle East, it needs to be considered that beside the fact that pricing tends to be erratic, they are also often not available. In addition, a strong tendency to respond to news can be observed from these issues. For example, when in November 2009 Dubai World announced a six-month payment holiday on all debt including Nakheel's $3.5 billion *sukuk,* prices of all *sukuk* showed a dramatic drop. Interestingly, there was no real impact on the conventional bond market, even though only 30 per cent of the underlying debt was financed in a *Sharia'a*-compliant manner, with the remaining 70 per cent being conventional finance.

5.6.3 Independent verification

Once the administrator has determined the fund value as well as the value per unit, the initial results are sent to the fund's accountants and the fund manager for verification. Any discrepancies with expected values are queried

Figure 5.5 *Sukuk pricing*

and only when the verification process is complete are the valuations finalised by the administrator.

5.6.4 Publication

Once the asset valuations and the net asset value per share is approved, the administrator officially publishes the values.

5.7 Prospecting and marketing

In order to attract investors, the fund provides marketing material and publishes fact sheets on a regular basis. Advertising, public speaking at conferences and brochures are all part of the marketing effort to attract investors. Western regulators dictate that when publishing marketing material, the fund and its sponsors will have to ensure that the content is true, fair and not misleading. Performance figures will have to be determined using acceptable standards and commentary must not use any suggestive language. Generally, marketing departments or companies ensure the design of all material is in line with company branding, and the compliance officer will ensure the content is written in such a way that it meets the regulatory rules and regulations.

In the end, however, the success of a *Sharia'a*-compliant fund in attracting funds is generally based on the same criteria as a conventional fund. The investor's perception of the strength of the fund manager, the distributor, the liquidity agent and the fund's track record are all important elements for an investor to consider.

5.8 Liquidity management

Liquidity is generally defined as the ability to fund the purchasing of assets and to meet obligations as they come due. In order to be able to meet the liquidity requirements, a financial institution holds cash as well as other assets that can be converted into cash at short notice without significant loss. The latter are often also defined as near-cash. Essentially, liquidity represents the requirement to have cash available as and when it is needed for example in order to meet redemption requests. Similar to any other financial institution, funds need to maintain a level of liquidity commensurate with their strategy and fund characteristics.

Liquidity management is a significant part a fund manager's job, since the fund manager's ability to redeem investments is essential to ensure investor comfort. There is however a cost associated with maintaining significant levels of liquidity which has a direct impact on profitability. Maintaining the balance between liquidity and profitability is not an easy task, but is aided by a number of characteristics that can be defined at the fund level such as gates, minimum holding periods and the repayment period.

Policies and procedures need to be in place for each of

the funds regarding the management of liquidity and the liquidity strategy of the fund. Liquidity is an important factor in a fund in so much that it provides the opportunity to redeem funds on a client's request. However, liquid funds are typically invested in short-term cash-like assets which, although relatively low risk, typically have a low level of return. Additional costs such as a higher aggregate transaction cost due to the short-term nature of the assets also have a negative impact on profitability. This trade-off between liquidity and profitability needs to be carefully managed by the fund manager to ensure that on the one hand profitability is as high as possible, whilst on the other hand still being able to maintain the desired liquidity position.

The liquidity strategy needs to be well known to those involved in the management of the fund. Investors need to be aware of the liquidity levels in the fund and potential limitations to redemptions in order for them to make an informed decision regarding investment in the fund. The accountant will, on a regular basis, report the liquidity position of the fund and specifically notifies any current or expected breaches in limits.

The liquidity strategy and policies will need to be reviewed on a regular basis to ensure they remain fit for purpose and to make amendments if necessary. One of the key elements of liquidity management is the use of scenario analysis to determine whether the implemented liquidity strategy is sufficient to cater for exceptional circumstances.

Directly associated with liquidity requirements are liquidity risks which are typically categorised into four types as follows:

1. **Funding liquidity risk.** This is the risk that the fund will be unable to meet its redemption obligations within the stated timeframe because of a shortage of liquid assets,

an inability to liquidate assets at a reasonable cost or to obtain adequate outside funding at an acceptable price. This is further extended to an inability to maintain or acquire sufficient funds in a crisis such as the 2008/2009 credit crisis.

2. **Market liquidity risk.** The risk that a specific exposure cannot be unwound or offset without a significant impact on market prices as a result of inadequate market depth or market disruptions is known as market liquidity risk. The nature of this risk can be cyclical or the result of market disruption.

3. **Mismatch or structural risk.** Financial institutions typically tend to attract short-term placements versus long-term liabilities. The maturity mismatch thus created results in mismatch or structural risk, as there is a chance that funds placed with the bank may be withdrawn prior to the liability maturing.

4. **Contingency risk.** Situations may occur where the need for liquid assets is larger than originally projected. Although contingency risk is mainly associated with banking operations, they could occasionally occur in asset management operations for instance due to a simultaneous redemption by multiple investors which is in excess of what would be expected.

All of these risks are associated with financial institutions in general, but are equally applicable to Islamic financial institutions as well as Islamic asset management operations.

Liquidity is typically managed by the fund manager in combination with the overall strategy of the fund. Depending on the size of the organisation and the size of the fund, the fund manager can either place liquid assets themselves or make use of a dedicated dealing room function. The latter is typically applied in large asset management companies or where the asset management division is part of a bank.

The main sources of liquidity for *Sharia'a*-compliant institutions are cash, commodity *murabaha* and *wakala*.

- **Cash** is generally held in non-interest bearing current accounts either with conventional or Islamic financial institutions. Although cash is a strong defensive element, the disadvantage in holding large cash balances is that they are counterproductive since they do not generate a return.
- **Commodity *murabaha* or *tawarruq*** can be used for longer- and shorter-term interbank placements as described in detail in section 2.5.4. Due to the fixed mark-up, the transactions are generally entered into for medium to short term. Although designed to synthesise interbank placements, commodity *murabaha* and *tawarruq* transactions have an additional cost associated with them for the purchase and sale of the metal warrants which signify the ownership of the asset. These costs, around 25 US dollars per million, can be prohibitive for short-dated transactions.
- ***Wakala*** is, like commodity *murabaha* and *tawarruq*, generally used for interbank placements although most *Sharia'a*-compliant institutions would only place funds by means of a *wakala* transaction with other Islamic financial institutions since the proceeds from conventional banks cannot be guaranteed to be *Sharia'a* compliant.
- **Other funds** can be invested in to provide short-term liquidity against a return. It needs to be considered that funds may have a minimum subscription period during which the funds cannot be redeemed.

Overnight and periodic investment programmes which are generally available in the conventional market have so far not yet developed in the Islamic finance market.

5.9 Risk management

The ethical framework governing Islamic finance prohibits gambling, uncertainty and interest, which leads to the initial impression that *Sharia'a*-compliant funds and financial institutions run little to no risk. This is however not the case and, like other banks and financial institutions, Islamic financial institutions face risks inherent to the financial industry, and in most countries they have to abide by the same rules as other financial institutions for the calculation of regulatory capital. In addition, there is a set of additional risks that applies to *Sharia'a*-compliant financial institutions. Conventional banks are subject to a wide range of risks, described in Table 5.1.

The need to quantify these risks has resulted in the development of what is currently the most widely used risk measure for banks, value at risk (VaR). In fund management, VaR can be used to attempt to measure the downside risk of the portfolio taking into account financial leverage and diversification effects. The result of the VaR equation is represented in the maximum amount the fund is likely to stand to lose on a given day or over a number of days (for example, over a period of one week), generally with a confidence interval of 95 or 99 per cent.

The absence of interest, and hence of interest rate risk as such, does not imply that a *Sharia'a*-compliant fund can be considered to bear lower levels of risk. Like conventional funds, *Sharia'a*-compliant funds incur liquidity, credit, settlement, leverage, operational and business risk. In addition there are a number of other types of risk run by

Table 5.1 *Types of risk for conventional banks*

Type of risk	Description
Liquidity risk	The risk of insufficient liquidity for normal operating requirements, that is, the ability of the bank to meet its liabilities when they fall due.
Interest rate risk	The risk arising from interest rate mismatches in volume, maturity and type (fixed vs floating) of interest-sensitive assets, liabilities and off-balance sheet items.
Credit risk	The risk that an asset or a loan becomes irrecoverable in the case of outright default, or the risk of delay in the servicing of the loan.
Settlement or counterparty risk	The risk that occurs if one party to a transaction pays funds or delivers assets prior to receiving its own funds or assets, hence exposing it to a potential loss.
Price risk	The risk that the market price of an instrument traded in a well-defined market will be volatile. Market risk occurs in relation to debt securities, derivatives, equity derivatives and currency transactions held by a bank.
Leverage risk (capital adequacy)	The risk related to the extent to which the assets of a bank may decline before the positions of its depositors and other creditors are jeopardised.
Event or operational risk	The risk of certain events occurring, for example disaster, regulatory or political events, or the (temporary) unavailability of IT systems.
Business risk	The risks related to products, macro-economic cycles and technology changes.

Sharia'a-compliant funds in the form of changes in asset and liability returns and value, due to changing economic circumstances affecting the investments that are part of the portfolio. Instead of fixed-rate interest rate risk, which is a balance sheet (fair value) exposure, *Sharia'a*-compliant funds face a rate of return risk, which is an income statement (cash flow) exposure, similar in nature to floating-rate interest rate risk in conventional funds. Rate of return risk is mainly related to sale-based instruments such as *murabaha*, *salam*, and *istisna* as well as *ijara* instruments. Although the risks are considered to be small for short-term *murabaha* contracts, the risk increases for transactions with a longer maturity. One of the risk mitigation techniques in use is to link *ijara* rentals to a benchmark such as LIBOR or an inflation index and periodically adjust the rental amounts.

In order to measure the risk of a *Sharia'a* compliant fund properly, the applicable risks need to be taken into consideration, and need to include risk types that cater specifically for the risks undertaken by Islamic financial institutions, such as:

- **Fiduciary risk.** Specifically, risk related to the nature of the *mudaraba* contract, which places liability for losses on the *mudarib* (or agent) in the case of malfeasance, negligence or breach of contract on the part of the management of the *mudaraba*.
- **Displaced commercial risk.** This risk type is related to the common practice among Islamic banks of "smoothing" the financial returns to investment account holders by varying the percentage of profit taken as the *mudarib* share, which can be compared to an arrangement or agency fee.
- **Rate of return risk.** The risk of a mismatch between yields on assets and the expected rates of both restricted

and unrestricted investment accounts which may in turn lead to displaced commercial risk. (Archer and Karim 2006)

Generally, the differences between the operations of conventional and *Sharia'a*-compliant funds result in a different level of risk. The riskiness of *Sharia'a*-compliant institutions is perceived to be higher than conventional institutions, for instance due to the profit- and loss-sharing modes of financing and the related increased potential for moral hazard, the potential incentive for risk taking without adequate capital levels, the lower levels of risk hedging instruments and techniques, and underdeveloped or non-existent capital markets. A significant part of the higher perceived risk levels is, however, associated with the fact that most *Sharia'a*-compliant funds and their investments are based in jurisdictions that are considered to be emerging markets. With Islamic finance gaining popularity in the Western world, more banks and funds are starting to operate out of financial centres such as London, Luxembourg and Ireland. These institutions need to be authorised and regulated by Western financial regulators and will have to compete in a rounded financial environment. The risk levels of these *Sharia'a*-compliant financial institutions are not higher than those of their conventional counterparts, and could even be considered lower due to the absence of speculative instruments that caused such disruption in the financial markets around the end of 2008 and have an ongoing impact on the global economy.

The risks taken by a *Sharia'a*-compliant fund are managed in a variety of ways, and will need to remain within the remit of the investment mandate as defined at the outset of the fund incorporation. The measures include, but are not restricted to:

- **Limit breaches.** Controls on limit breaches are monitored by the back office and reported to the relevant parties for the appropriate action to be taken. This includes breaches that occur for instance as a result of changes in exchange rates.
- **Credit rating changes.** In the event an issuer or counterparty is downgraded to a level below the acceptable level identified in the investment mandate, the investment needs to be unwound. Unlike conventional funds, a *Sharia'a*-compliant fund is not allowed to purchase credit protection such as credit default swaps (CDS) due to the fact that they are used speculatively.
- **Asset allocation.** The asset allocations identified in the investment mandate are put in place to control the risk levels of the investments. In addition, asset allocation is used to ensure diversification in the portfolio and that liquidity requirements can be met.

Each of these measures does not significantly differ from those applied in conventional fund management with the exception that all instruments applied for investment management as well as to control its risks need to be *Sharia'a* compliant. It is, in this respect, worth noting again that the investment mandate of a *Sharia'a*-compliant fund specifically stipulates the guidelines for *Sharia'a* compliance by which the fund needs to abide.

Notes

1. Norges Bank Investment Management Investment Mandate, Section 2: General Constraints, http://www.norges-bank.no/upload/78306/nbim%20public%20investment%20mandate%20spu%20dec09.pdf (accessed 24 March 2010).
2. Durban Pension Fund Investment Policy Document, Section 9: General Constraints, http://www.durban.gov.za/urban/

government/treasury/pensions/investment-policy/investment-policy.pdf (accessed 24 March 2010).

3. Al Rajhi Global Small Cap Equity Fund Investment Mandate, http://www.alrajhi-capital.com/NR/rdonlyres/BBE66546-78F7-40E8-A86C-1E288365C478/193/SmallCapBrochureContentsdated0108091.pdf (accessed 24 March 2010).

CHAPTER 6
SHARIA'A SUPERVISORY BOARD

The *Sharia'a* supervisory board (SSB) plays an important role in any Islamic financial institution. Although the principles underlying fund management as outlined in the previous chapters are universally applicable and are not restricted to conventional funds, *Sharia'a*-compliant funds have to abide by the rules of *Sharia'a* as stipulated in their investment mandate. The requirement for all financial structures, products and transactions applied in *Sharia'a*-compliant asset management to be *Sharia'a* compliant ensures that specific religious aspects are met which is important for two distinct parties: the Islamic asset management firm or division and the fund investors. The firm needs to ensure that products and instruments offered are genuinely *Sharia'a* compliant and in line with their standards, principles and shareholder demands. Investors need to ensure that the offering satisfies their requirements and is in line with their own religious beliefs.

In line with the exponential growth of the Islamic finance industry over the past few decades, the role of the SSB has also evolved. Initially financial institutions would turn to scholars specialising in Islamic law and jurisprudence who would opine on the eligibility of a product or service. Increasingly, however, scholars have also developed a strong background in business and finance and they are becoming more involved in the earlier stages of product development.

The roles and responsibilities, the different functions of the board, the mechanics of selecting the board, governance issues, challenges and some specific issues in asset management are outlined in the remainder of this chapter.

6.1 Roles of the *Sharia'a* supervisory board

The role of the SSB can generally be divided into three distinct areas: advisory, approval and audit. Not only does each of these areas have its own set of Islamic jurisprudence guidelines which may depend on the different schools of thought, but also there are industry standards and local regulations to conform to such as the industry standards published by the Accounting and Auditing Organization for Islamic Financial Institutions (AAOIFI) and the rule books published by respective local regulators. This section explores the different roles of the SSB in more detail.

6.1.1 Advisory role

On many occasions a conventional or an Islamic financial institution can be seeking generic advice on the treatment of a matter which is governed by *Sharia'a* principles. This is not necessarily related to a particular instrument but could, for example, be related to staff or maintenance contracts. In these cases, the SSB would be able to provide advice. However, as the financial institution becomes larger, it would be considered best practice to either employ an in-house *Sharia'a* specialist or an employee with in-depth knowledge of *Sharia'a* teachings who could fulfil a generic, first-line advisory role where required. Besides providing a continuous level of service, in-house expertise enhances the availability of *Sharia'a*-related knowledge within the institution and improves the effectiveness and efficiency of the SSB since they will not have to deal with the more mundane aspects to the same extent. It enables the SSB to focus on the more unusual challenges, innovation and improvement of transaction types hence achieving maximum utilisation and productivity of the SSB. *Sharia'a*-compliant funds typically do not employ their own in-house expert which is mainly due to their size in combination with the fact that the instruments they apply are generally fairly generic.

6.1.2 Approval role

The approval role of the SSB focuses on the approval of financial instruments and structures the Islamic financial institution offers to client. The process itself can be defined in six different steps which take the process from the review of the initial structure to the final approval and implementation. Figure 6.1 illustrates the generally accepted best practice for the process of approving a new product or instrument.

1. **Product structuring.** The initial thought process leading to the development of a new product is typically driven by client demand. Depending on the type of institution, this could be based on market research (a process more applicable for retail and highly standardised instruments) or to meet the demand for a particular financing requirement (a process more applicable in wholesale and investment banking or for highly individual instruments).

2. **Product or concept approval.** Once the initial concept is defined in sufficient detail, it is presented to the SSB for review and to ensure *Sharia'a* compliance. The result of the review process is either initial approval or results in further discussions regarding areas where the concept

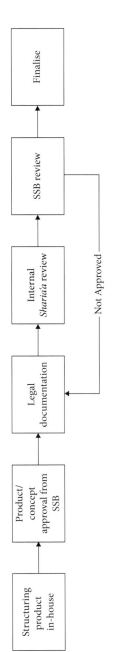

Figure 6.1 Sharia'a *approval process for a new product or structure*

may face challenges in achieving *Sharia'a* compliance. The process is highly unlikely to result in a definitive rejection. The structure is likely to have at least checked that the basic *Sharia'a* tenets are not violated, although further fine tuning may be required. It is important to bear in mind that this is an iterative process, and effective communication between the structurer and the SSB is important to achieve an instrument that is *Sharia'a* compliant whilst at the same time meeting the client's and fund manager's requirements.

3. **Legal documentation.** Once the concept is approved by the SSB, the legal documentation will be drawn up, or reviewed when it concerns an investment in an instrument offered by another institution. This is typically done by the institution's in-house legal team who will seek outside counsel if required.

4. **Internal** *Sharia'a* **review.** Once the legal documentation is completed, the in-house *Sharia'a* expert will review the documentation to ensure there are no obvious challenges which could result in non-compliance of the contract.

5. **SSB review.** Upon completion of the internal review, the draft legal structure will be provided to the SSB for review. The process to obtain approval for the legal documentation may require several iterations, and may have to be referred back to the legal team for further amendments.

6. **Finalise.** Once final approval has been obtained, the legal documentation is finalised and can be provided to the counterparty.

The approval process outlined here may vary on a transaction-by-transaction basis. Retail oriented products such as, for example, personal loans and credit cards need only be approved once and upon a change of the terms and conditions. Transactions in the wholesale and investment banking areas as well as wealth management transactions are often more individual in nature and can be more complex structures which will need to be reviewed on a transaction-by-transaction basis. *Sharia'a*-compliant fund management investments are typically reasonably homogenous, and the process to obtain *Sharia'a* approval is generally related to the review of investments already in existence.

It is worth emphasising that approval of the structure does not automatically result in approval of the legal documentation. The legal documentation may, for example, contain a non-compliant clause or condition or may vary from the original structure in such a way that compliance is no longer achieved. It is therefore important that the institution and its SSB remain diligent in their review process and take the utmost care when issuing *fatwas* to ensure that both the structure and the associated legal documentation are compliant.

Changes to existing structures that have previously been approved

Over time there is a reasonable likelihood that a previously approved structure will requires changes. This process is, depending on the extent of the changes, typically shorter and can be depicted as in Figure 6.2.

- **Propose product changes.** Any changes to an existing product need to be described in sufficient detail and presented to the SSB.

Figure 6.2 Sharia'a *approval process for changes to an existing product or structure*

- **SSB review.** The changes are reviewed to ensure the product remains *Sharia'a* compliant. In the event a change causes (part of) the product to become non-compliant, the SSB will provide comments and recommended changes to the product development team for their review. This process may go through several iterations in order to ensure the changes are approved. Typically, the changes to the product and the legal documentation are reviewed as one.
- **Finalise.** Once final approval has been obtained, the changes to the legal documentation are finalised and the product can be offered to clients.

6.1.3 Audit role

Besides the approval of new transactions and instruments, the SSB is often also involved in the *Sharia'a* compliance audit. In this role, the SSB is responsible for ensuring that all transactions the fund has entered into are indeed complying with the SSB guidelines and associated *fatwas*. Typically this is done by reviewing a significant sample of executed transactions, the *fatwas,* and any other guidelines issued. In addition, they also review other operations and expenses of the fund to ensure *Sharia'a* compliance within the general operational environment. The audit process itself differs per institution but the general characteristics are as follows:

- **Periodicity.** The periodicity of the audit depends on the size of the fund and the number of transactions entered into in a particular period. Typically, audits are quarterly, semi-annual or annual with the majority of the funds opting for semi-annual.
- **Organisation.** The scope of the audit covers all aspects of the fund's organisation.

Findings are reported to the fund's board of directors who are ultimately responsible for compliance with *Sharia'a*. It needs to be considered that in the event of non-compliance the fund can be found negligent which has severe implications for its ability to pass on potential losses to investors.[1]

6.1.4 Segregation of approval and audit

Where the approval role is often referred to as 'ex-ante' compliance due to its nature of providing approval prior to execution, the audit role is designed to ensure 'ex-post', or after the fact, compliance. It is currently accepted practice that both roles are executed by the SSB, although there are some proponents for segregation between the approval and the audit functions. As identified in more detail below, the advantages of having both roles reside with the SSB is that it is an efficient use of time since they are fully aware of the circumstances of the approval. However, audit requires a special skill set which is not necessarily within the capability of the SSB. In addition, where both roles reside with the SSB, this will put an additional strain on the often already hectic schedules of the *Sharia'a* scholars.

In any case, even when the audit function is executed by another party, the ultimate responsibility for checking *Sharia'a* compliance lies with the SSB. Each of these approaches has its advantages and disadvantages.

Ex-ante and ex-post compliance by the SSB
The SSB is fully aware of the developments in the institution and knows the underlying reasons for the approval or rejection of different contracts and instruments. As a result, on the one hand the SSB tends to be in a better position to judge whether or not the institution has been compliant with the guidelines hence providing an effective and efficient

process. On the other hand, having set the guidelines and issued the *fatwas* the SSB will have a pre-conceived idea of what it is looking for, therefore may be at a higher risk of overlooking something.

Ex-ante compliance by the SSB, ex-post by a separate function

The advantages of segregating these functions are two-fold. Firstly, audit is a particular skill with its own requirements. Secondly, by segregating the ex-ante and ex-post functions, scholars' precious time will be released which will reduce one of the main current bottlenecks: the availability of sufficient experienced scholars. The disadvantage of this approach is that the auditor may either not fully appreciate or understand a guideline or *fatwa* or, in the worst case, may argue the correctness of the guideline or *fatwa* itself.

6.2 Social responsibilities

The role of the SSB is not limited to fulfilling its function within the confines of the fund, but extends to the application of the ethical principles and hence to the implementation of Islamic structures from a social perspective. There are different ways in which the SSB is involved in social responsibilities, one of them being *zakat* or mandatory charitable giving. The SSB is responsible for the calculation of *zakat* obligations on a per-share basis, irrespective of whether the fund pays *zakat* directly or has delegated this responsibility to the investors in the fund. Although *zakat* is a mechanism of wealth purification, it more importantly is seen as a means of redistributing income, which results in a reduction of social and economic inequality. The role of the SSB in calculating the investors' *zakat* contribution is therefore regarded as a social responsibility for the benefit of society as a whole. In addition to *zakat*, the SSB will also ensure and supervise that any penalty payments paid to the fund are directed to a charity, or scientific or educational cause. This will also be the case with any non-*Sharia'a*-compliant revenue.

In addition, the members of the SSB have, as an extension of their approval role, an obligation to ensure that the ethical principles outlined in *Sharia'a* are abided by. It is in this role that they contribute to the development of the Islamic financial industry in general and existing and contemporary products in particular. As such they provide a valuable contribution to the industry, and are at the centre of all developments and debates.

A further aspect of social responsibility is associated with maintaining confidence in the industry as well as the individual institutions and funds. As has become clear from the 2008/2009 global financial crisis, reputational risk is an important element of the financial industry. This is probably even more so for the Islamic financial industry due to its relatively short history and comparative size of the industry as a cross-section of the global financial industry. All these and other factors result in a stronger requirement for investor comfort. Particularly to those who invest in or transact with Islamic financial institutions on the basis of either their beliefs or the attractions of the underlying ethical framework, it is important to be able to rely on the opinions and advice of the SSB. It is the duty of the SSB to ensure the bank's reputation remains intact by maintaining best practice.

6.3 Corporate governance

The corporate governance structure of *Sharia'a*-compliant funds is similar to the structure of its conventional counterparts outlined in section 4.4 with the exception of the fact that *Sharia'a*-compliant funds have an additional mechanism of governance in the SSB.

Similar to conventional financial institutions, Islamic financial institutions and fund management companies typically have a supervisory board which consists of non-executive directors and a lower or executive board consisting of senior management and chaired by the CEO. Remuneration committees, audit committees and risk committees are all standard components of the governance structure.

In addition, Islamic financial institutions also have an SSB as part of the governance structure, whose role it is to ensure that the organisation is and remains *Sharia'a* compliant. The SSB reports to the supervisory board and works closely with the in-house legal team or *Sharia'a* advisor on new transactions and the review of new contracts with third-party suppliers. Five key characteristics of the SSB can be identified:

1. **Independence.** It is fundamental to the working of the SSB that it, as well as its members, is independent from the management of the institution. In order to ensure independence of the SSB the members are typically not appointed by the management of the financial institution but instead by the shareholders at the annual general meeting.

2. **Confidentiality.** *Sharia'a* scholars typically sit on multiple boards and are, as a result, exposed to significant amounts of proprietary information. Maintaining confidentiality is therefore of the utmost importance both for the board members and for the financial institutions on whose boards they serve.

3. **Competence.** As described in the section above, the

SSB and its members fulfil multiple roles. Not only are they expected to have specialist *Sharia'a* knowledge and expertise, in particular of *fiqh al muamalat* (Islamic law of contracts), but they are also required to have an understanding and knowledge of modern financial practices and products.

4. **Consistence.** Although it is recognised that best practice may change over time, decisions, guidelines and the advice of the SSB should be consistent in nature. This will assist in building up and maintaining consumer confidence, which is an important requirement, mutually beneficial for both the client and the financial institution.

5. **Disclosure.** Given the importance of *ijtihad* (interpretation) in the decision making process, disclosure and transparency surrounding procedures, decisions, *fatwa* and structural details are of vital importance. Enhanced transparency by the SSB encourages and promotes confidence in the financial institution and the wider industry for all stakeholders.

Each of the above elements needs to be considered in the implementation of the SSB within the corporate governance framework of an Islamic financial institution. Not only are they instrumental to the workings of the SSB, but in addition these are an integral part of its role within the growing Islamic financial industry.

6.4 Structures and variations of *Sharia'a* supervisory boards

The characteristics of the SSB and its members depend on the individual institution and the way it structures its Islamic financial services offering. When it comes to the principles of Islamic finance the differences of opinion between the different schools of thought in Islam are fairly insignificant. However, many Muslims tend to follow a particular school of thought and consequently tend to extend this to their choice of financial product. From the *Sharia'a*-compliant fund manager's perspective, it is therefore of importance to choose the members of the SSB in such a way that they represent the majority views of the geographic location where the majority of its target investor base is located. This is particularly true in countries where, incidentally, the majority of the Muslim population follows the same school of thought, such as the *Hanafi* in Pakistan, the *Shafi'i* in Malaysia and the *Hanbali* in Saudi Arabia. In these countries investors are less likely to invest if the product has not been approved by a *Sharia'a* board that consists of at least one scholar of the particular school of thought they follow. In order to overcome this, or restrict themselves to a single geographical area, Islamic financial institutions typically select the scholars that make up their SSB from different schools of thought, thus providing a broad range of clients with the reassurance and comfort they require.

However, having scholars from different schools of thought on one board inevitably leads to more discussion on some of the detailed characteristics of an individual instrument which is beneficial to the end result and the acceptability of a product or transaction by a wider audience. It is therefore important to find the right balance between the scholars to obtain a balanced, consensus view on acceptability of an instrument or individual structure.

When selecting the members of the SSB, their background, other commitments and accessibility are important factors. Accessibility is particularly important since it is vital in the development of the long-term relationship between the board and the institution. Not only does it ensure effective and efficient operating, it also enhances the overall value the institution can offer and the effective use of resources.

Although these factors are certainly widely accepted and considered, the actual implementation varies. In the market, the following main trends are seen:

- Central SSB on which each school of thought is represented in combination with regional sub-SSBs comprised of regional scholars representing the regional consensus interpretation. This structure is particularly suitable for large institutions with a global presence.
- Single (exclusive) scholar highly respected and reputable in the country of operation. This approach typically only works for banks operating in a single jurisdiction and will provide continuous access to the scholar.
- Appoint local scholars as opposed to internationally well-known scholars. Although the scholars might be less well known they are also less likely to be overstretched in their commitments and may therefore be able to give more time and attention. In addition, it will increase the number of experienced scholars in the industry.
- Create a further executive committee within the SSB composed of, for example, two members with the additional responsibility to act on behalf of the SSB on urgent matters and who assume delegation on certain issues. The executive committee typically includes the chair of the SSB.

The number of scholars appointed to the SSB varies from institution to institution. AAOIFI's standard on the SSB asks for a minimum of three scholars to be appointed, although in practice there does not appear to be any significant conflict between the AAOIFI standard and any alternative approaches such as the single dedicated scholar as described above. Islamic financial institutions opting for a smaller SSB generally chose to do so for a variety of reasons such as the size of the organisation, the amount of business they conduct or because they are part of a larger organisation with a central SSB.

6.5 Challenges facing *Sharia'a* supervisory boards

One of the main challenges facing the Islamic financial industry is associated with the relative scarcity of scholars who can combine an understanding of *Sharia'a* principles, *fiqh al muamalat* and financial products and services. The number of scholars that have a combination of these skills are scarce and highly sought after. As a result, the same highly qualified scholars sit on many different boards, a situation which often attracts significant criticism. There are, however, valid reasons for this situation:

- The more experience a scholar gains in the financial services industry, the more they will be in demand, which in turn increases their experience thus creating a vicious circle.
- The specialist knowledge required in the areas of *Sharia'a* and *fiqh al muamalat* takes a long time to accumulate and the consequent lack of resources reinforces the challenges associated with obtaining sufficient experience.

Recent initiatives such as the AAOIFI *Sharia'a* advisor and audit qualifications are attempting to address the shortage of qualifications for practitioners. Qualified *Sharia'a* auditors could for example take over some of the SSB audit tasks thus freeing up some of the scholars' time while also enhancing the overall level of knowledge and experience throughout the Islamic financial industry.

Further harmonisation of industry standards also takes some of the pressure off the *Sharia'a* scholars since not every individual transaction needs to be reviewed in detail.

6.6 *Sharia'a* supervisory boards in asset management

The SSB for a fund is appointed prior to the incorporation of the fund by the board of directors. Similar to other Islamic financial institutions, the SSB is responsible for defining the *Sharia'a* parameters that apply given the overall fund investment strategy. The SSB for a *Sharia'a*-compliant fund typically consists of two to five members, who can be a subset of the scholars appointed to the SSB of the fund management company or the financial institution it is a part of. Disregarding how the SSB is constructed, it is generally deemed to be good practice for a fund to have its own board. Although specialist knowledge of the products the fund invests in would be recommended, it is not necessary in itself.

The *Sharia'a* parameters may vary by fund type and need to be adhered to by all parties. The ultimate responsibility for *Sharia'a* compliance lies with the board of directors, and non compliance could result in negligence which can have severe repercussions, particularly where *mudaraba* transactions are involved in which case the *mudarib* becomes responsible for all losses and will not be able to pass them on to the investors.

The parameters defined by the SSB are purely associated with *Sharia'a* compliance, and are communicated to the investors via the offering memorandum and potentially other material. On a regular basis, typically quarterly or semi-annually, the SSB convenes to audit the fund on *Sharia'a* compliance and to opine on any new transaction types.

It needs to be emphasised however that opining on the suitability of an individual investment beyond its *Sharia'a* compliance is outside the scope of the SSB. The fund manager makes all investment decisions, and although the SSB may make the fund manager aware of a particular investment opportunity, there is no obligation on the part of the manager to actually invest in this. To the contrary, investing in any asset without due process would be considered contradictory to prudent investment procedures.

Reviewing the SSB of the different *Sharia'a* index providers, for example, provides some insight into how the boards are constructed. Most index providers have an SSB of four scholars, with one of them having five. Some boards share the same scholars, with two of them sitting on four different boards, one on three and one on two different boards. However, out of the 12 scholars that make up the five different boards, the vast majority (that is, eight) sit only on one individual board. This is fairly representative for SSBs across the Islamic financial industry, where few scholars sit on many different boards, supplemented by others who might be newer to the industry and sit only on a few boards.

The SSB meets generally between two and four times per year to review different products and contracts, but it is important to bear in mind that the SSB defines the *Sharia'a* compliance guidelines for the investment mandate, but does not have a final say in whether or not to invest in a particular instrument as long as it is within the rules outlined in the investment mandate.

6.7 Non-compliant investments

Particularly where equity investments are concerned, it is possible that, due to for example adverse market conditions, an investment becomes temporarily non-compliant. Upon incorporation of the fund, the SSB will have defined the regulation for this, which could for example indicate that a short period of non-compliance is allowed, or that an immediate divestment process needs to be started. Divestment is typically allowed to occur over a period of time to ensure that investors are not unnecessarily disadvantaged in the process. Any income from non-compliant investments will need to be purified via charitable contributions.

Note

1. Where funds are made available to the fund under a *mudaraba* structure, the fund, in its capacity of *mudarib*, is not responsible for any losses unless they are proven to be negligent in which case they are responsible for the total losses occurred.

CHAPTER 7

CASE STUDIES

This chapter provides case studies of a select number of *Sharia'a*-compliant funds. These funds have been randomly selected based on their type and geography and their inclusion here does not represent an endorsement, investment advice, or that they are better or worse than any of the other funds available in the market when it comes to *Sharia'a* compliance or performance.

When making an investment decision, investors will have to satisfy themselves that their requirements, including but not restricted to their risk appetite and the goodness of fit of the fund within their overall portfolio, are met. When investing in *Sharia'a*-compliant funds, the investor also needs to ensure that the fund's framework for *Sharia'a* compliance meets the investor's own requirements. In any case investors will always need to bear in mind that past performance is no indication for the future.

The information presented in the case studies is publicly available from a variety of sources such as web sites, press releases, fact sheets and databases as well as offering memoranda and the fund prospectus. A similar structure is applied for each of the case studies, providing a little background on the fund manager, fund objectives, asset allocation and performance.

7.1 Fixed Income Fund: the BLME $ Income Fund

As detailed in section 3.2, the asset allocation of fixed income type funds dictates the risk–return profile and has an impact on the liquidity of the fund. The example used in this case study is the $ income compartment of the Umbrella Fund SICAV-SIF, from Bank of London and The Middle East plc (BLME), whose asset management division manages the fund.

Background on the asset manager
BLME is incorporated in the United Kingdom and was authorised by the UK Financial Services Authority (FSA) as a fully *Sharia'a*-compliant investment bank in July 2007. The bank offers asset management via one of its divisions and in 2009 the first compartment of the Umbrella Fund SICAV-SIF was launched.

Jurisdiction of incorporation
The umbrella fund is incorporated as a *société d'investissement à capital variable*-specialised investment fund (SICAV-SIF) in Luxembourg and is regulated by the *Commission de Surveillance du Secteur Financier* (CSSF), Luxembourg's financial supervisory authority.

There are a number of advantages to incorporating in Luxembourg, which can be summarised as follows:

- **Regulation.** The fund will be regulated under European and international standards. Typically, the fact that a fund is regulated under international standards enhances investor comfort and may assist in attracting investors from a larger range of jurisdictions. In addition, one of the control criteria for incorporation as a SICAV-SIF is that the fund's custodian needs to be a bank or financial institution regulated in Luxembourg.

- **Qualifying assets.** The governing law does not place any restriction on the nature of the assets the fund can invest in. Not only does that leave the fund free to invest in non-conventional asset types such as *sukuk*, but it also allows for new products and instruments to be considered for inclusion in the fund as they may become available. Particularly in a fast-growing industry where new instruments are likely to be developed this is a significant advantage.

- **Tax regime.** Under the Luxembourg regulations, a SIF is exempt from the payment of income tax, capital gains tax, withholding tax and VAT, although the latter is only associated with the management charges. In the event the SIF is established as a company it will, however, be subject to a capital duty on formation or increase of capital. The largely tax exempt status results in a situation where the investor is only liable for the taxation in their own jurisdiction, regardless of whether or not a tax treaty is in place which in turn means that there is no unnecessary monetary disadvantage in investing in the fund.

The potential disadvantage of this structure is that SIF-based funds are only available for qualifying investors, which reduces the potential size of the investor base as these funds cannot, for example, be offered to retail investors. Under Luxembourg law,[1] a well-informed investor is identified as any one of the following:

- An institutional investor, defined as a bank or financial institution.
- A professional investor, being an investor that routinely

carries out financial transactions and could be a company or an individual.

- Any investor that meets the following two conditions: they attest in a duly signed document that they are a well-informed investor and the amount of the investment is at least €125,000; or an attestation is issued and signed by a bank or another financial institution confirming that the investor understands the SIF's investment and is able to assess the potential risks involved.

Fund objective

The fund objective is to invest in assets that are *Sharia'a* compliant, achieving a target gross return of three-month $ LIBOR plus one per cent per annum. The fund invests in short-term money market instruments such as *wakala* and commodity *murabaha* for liquidity purposes and longer-dated instruments such as *sukuk* and *ijara* to generate a return.

General fund characteristics

Any fund has a number of general characteristics such as currency, share classes, benchmark and redemptions. For the BLME $ Income Fund these characteristics are reported to be as follows:

- **Currency:** US dollar.
- **Share classes:** Six, each of which has a different minimum initial investment amount.
- *Sharia'a* **supervisory board members:** Two, both of whom are also on the *Sharia'a* supervisory board of BLME.
- **Redemptions:** Weekly.
- **Benchmark:** Three-month $ LIBOR.
- **Target return:** Three-month $ LIBOR plus 1 per cent.

- **Minimum investment:** $250,000.
- **Distribution policy:** Quarterly.
- **Management fees:** Ranging from 0.25 to 0.5 per cent per annum.
- ***Zakat* payment:** Responsibility of the investor.

In addition to these general characteristics, the fund's investment mandate stipulates specific characteristics for the individual assets. See Table 7.1.

Generic asset allocation

Although likely to vary on a periodic basis depending on market circumstances and expected liquidity requirements, the generic asset allocation for the BLME $ Income Fund, as per the fund factsheet dated 31 March 2010, can be represented as in Figure 7.1.[2]

When compared to the risk–return curve for fixed income-type funds described in section 3.2 and replicated in Figure 7.2, it becomes clear that the asset allocation of the $ Income Fund fits in between a fixed income-type fund and an enhanced cash fund, leaning more towards the enhanced cash-type structures. This type of structure generally has a medium risk and the potential to generate medium returns relative to other fixed income funds, bearing in mind that fixed income funds, unlike for example equity funds, are generally not particularly risky. In addition, as represented by the weekly redemption window, these funds may experience lower liquidity.

Generic geographical exposure

As a result of the overweighting in *sukuk*, the majority of the geographical exposure (approximately 60 to 70 per cent) is against the Gulf Cooperation Council (GCC), with the remainder spread globally. This situation is largely due to

Table 7.1 *Generic asset characteristics, BLME $ Income Fund*

Characteristic	Description
Permitted assets	Specification of the assets that the fund manager can include in the fund. In addition to the fact that all investments need to be *Sharia'a* compliant, specific instruments are listed which include, but are not restricted to, short-term placements, *sukuk*, *ijara* and other collective investment funds.
Liquidity	Specification of the minimum amount of funds that need to mature on the NAV date in order to meet potential liquidity requirements. This is expressed as a percentage of total assets.
Short-term yield pick up	Specification of a minimum amount of assets that need to mature over a short investment horizon. This is expressed as a percentage of total assets.
Maximum weightings	Specification of the maximum position per instrument that can be held in the fund as a percentage of total assets.
Ratings	Specification of the minimum credit rating per instrument or instrument type. Where possible, an external rating is used, but this can be supplemented with an internal rating. In the event an internal rating is used, additional criteria may be required related to issues such as the frequency and transparency of information.
Individual issuer exposure	Specification of restrictions on individual issuer or issuer-type exposure expressed as a percentage of the issue. Variations may apply for different types of issuer or ratings.
Ratings downgrade	Specification of the steps to be taken in the event of a ratings downgrade.

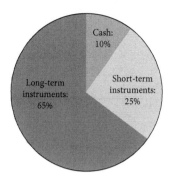

Figure 7.1 *BLME $ Income Fund target asset allocation*

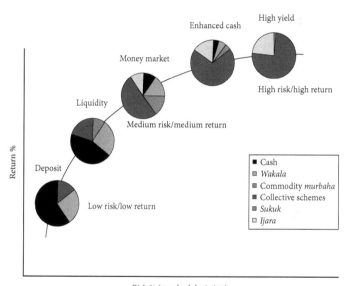

Figure 7.2 *Fixed income funds on the risk/return curve*

the fact that the majority of *sukuk* are issued by entities
in this region. However, with Islamic financial instruments
gaining momentum globally, this may change. Even so, the
holdings are highly diversified and incorporate different
credit qualities.

Performance

Providing up-to-date performance data is outside the scope of this book, and in any case an investor needs to be satisfied with the suitability of an investment to meet their needs prior to making an investment decision. Performance is subject to change due to, for instance, market circumstances, and developments internal to the fund. It is however notewor-thy that for its first year since launch, the fund was ranked in the top quartile of the Global Money Market peer group, as allocated by Lipper Hindsight. Although past performance is no indication of the future, the metric in itself shows that *Sharia'a*-compliant fixed income funds can indeed compete with conventional funds. The Global Money Market peer group contains around 900 fixed income-type funds with similar characteristics, of which, as of March 2010, 13 are flagged as *Sharia'a* compliant.

The fund has also outperformed its benchmark during its first year, even though the debt restructuring announce-ment of Dubai World in the fourth quarter of 2009, which did not have a direct impact on the fund (according to the factsheets there is no exposure to Dubai World),[3] severely depressed the performance of the overall *sukuk* market. Given the underlying securities, all funds with similar char-acteristics will be negatively effected by shocks in the market such as the announcement from the Dubai Government related to the debt restructuring of Dubai World. A longer investment time horizon will even out this type of volatility.

Conclusion

The BLME $ Income Fund clearly shows that *Sharia'a* compliance does not have to result in lower performance compared to conventional fixed income funds. To the con-trary, compared to its conventional peers, the fund has per-formed relatively well during its first year of incorporation even though market circumstances were not particularly favourable during the period. Clearly past performance is no indication of future performance and it could probably be argued that the peer group chosen by Lipper for the fund might not be fully representative. This issue is not unique to this fund but is experienced by many funds in this group. As new, more granular peer groups evolve, peer group analysis is likely to become more meaningful.

7.2 Equity Fund: SWIP Islamic Global Equity Fund

As detailed in section 3.6, equity funds are generally considered at the higher risk end of the fund spectrum since equity prices are generally more volatile, a situation that was made painfully clear by the severe reduction in equity prices after the bankruptcy of Lehman Brothers in September 2008. However, the higher risk may result in a potentially higher return.

The example used in this case study is the SWIP Islamic Global Equity Fund, managed by the Scottish Widows Investment Partnership (SWIP), which has an active investment strategy and measures itself against the Dow Jones Global Islamic Index.

Background on the asset manager
Scottish Widows Investment Partnership (SWIP) is one of Europe's largest asset management companies, is part of Lloyds Banking Group, and has a global presence. Incorporated and authorised in the United Kingdom, as of 31 December 2009 SWIP had assets under management of £141.72 billion, managed via a wide range of investment vehicles.[4] A conventional asset manager, SWIP introduced the SWIP Islamic Global Equity Fund in 2005 in response to opportunities in the market.

Jurisdiction of incorporation

The SWIP Islamic Global Equity Fund is incorporated as a *société d'investissement à capital variable* (SICAV) in Luxembourg and is regulated by the *Commission de Surveillance du Secteur Financier* (CSSF), Luxembourg's financial supervisory authority. The SICAV is governed by Part I of the law of 2002 which governs SICAVs in transferrable securities.

There are a number of advantages to incorporating in Luxembourg which can be summarised as follows:

- **Regulation.** The fund will be regulated to European and international standards. Typically, the fact that a fund is regulated to international standards enhances investor comfort, and in addition may assist in attracting investors from a larger range of jurisdictions. In addition, one of the control criteria for incorporation as a SICAV is that the fund's custodian needs to be a bank or financial institution regulated in Luxembourg.
- **Qualifying assets.** The governing law does not place any restriction on the nature of the assets the fund can invest in. Not only does that leave the fund free to invest in non-conventional asset types such as *sukuk*, but it also allows for new products and instruments to be considered for inclusion in the fund as they may become available. Particularly in a fast-growing industry where new instruments are likely to be developed, this is a significant advantage.
- **Tax regime.** Luxembourg-based investment vehicles are largely tax exempt, which results in a situation where the investor is only liable for the taxation in their own jurisdiction, regardless of whether or not a tax treaty is in place which in turn means that there is no unnecessary monetary disadvantage in investing in the fund.

The laws governing SICAV do not appear to restrict participation to particular investor groups. The SWIP Islamic Global Equity Fund itself, however, does and is open to professional or institutional clients only. In line with the MiFID definitions specified in section 4.4.1, these clients are categorised as follows:

- **Professional client.** An investor that routinely carries out financial transactions and could be a company or an individual.
- **Institutional client.** One of the most sophisticated counterparties and with the least protection. Insurance companies, funds, investment firms, central banks and financial institutions authorised and regulated by regulators either within or outside the EEA are among the types of institution that are automatically classified as eligible counterparties. In addition, corporate clients can be elected to be eligible counterparties if they fulfil a set number of criteria defined in the MiFID regulations.

Fund strategy

The fund is managed as a *Sharia'a* compliant high conviction equity portfolio, running a tracking error of 5 per cent against the Dow Jones Global Islamic Index.

Asset allocation and equity selection

The SWIP Islamic Global Equity Fund applies an active investment strategy and invests in public equity and equity-related transferable securities. For cash management purposes a combination of cash and exchange traded funds is used.

To achieve *Sharia'a* compliance the fund initially invested solely in assets that were part of the universe specified by the Dow Jones Global Islamic Index. In addition to these equities, the fund manager is actively seeking other opportunities to include in the investment universe. Once these are identified, they are initially screened by an Islamic stockbroker using a process which filters out any companies that do not meet the industry and financial screens, which are defined as follows:

- **Industry-related criteria.** Any corporation whose activities are against *Sharia'a* are excluded. The fund is therefore precluded from investing in companies in the following industries:
  - entertainment
  - tobacco
  - pork-related products
  - alcohol
  - conventional financial services
  - weapons and defence
  - sectors/companies significantly effected by the above.
- **Financial criteria.** In order to be eligible for incorporation in the investment universe, each of the following ratios must be below 33 per cent:
  - total debt / trailing 24-month average market capitalisation
  - (cash + interest bearing securities) / 24-month average market capitalisation
  - accounts receivable / 24-month average market capitalisation.

Once the equity has passed the screens outlined above, a proposal is drawn up for the fund's *Sharia'a* supervisory board, which further opines on the inclusion of the stock. This process is managed on an interactive basis and the decision follows thorough research combined with lengthy discussions between the Islamic stockbroker, the fund manager and the fund's *Sharia'a* supervisory board.

Any instrument that is part of the investment universe and becomes non-compliant will be removed from the universe. In the event the fund has invested in these equities, the fund manager will take all reasonable steps to dispose of the investment as soon as reasonably practicable, but always in the best interests of the investors. Disinvestment will take place over a period agreed by the *Sharia'a* supervisory board of the fund and is defined in the investment mandate.

Purification process

As a result of the fact that the fund invests in global public equity and even though the utmost care is taken in selecting the instruments that are part of the investment universe, a small proportion of the income could still be associated with conventional debt. Where this occurs, the fund purifies the relevant proportion of the income by deducting it from the net asset value and donating it to charity. The *Sharia'a* supervisory board determines which charities benefit from these proceeds.

General fund characteristics

Any fund has a number of general characteristics associated with the benchmark, share classes and redemptions. For the SWIP Islamic Global Equity Fund these characteristics are reported to be as follows:

- **Currency:** US dollar.
- **Share classes:** Three, each available in British pound, euro and US dollar.
- *Sharia'a* **supervisory board members:** Four.
- **Redemptions:** Daily on each business day.

- **Benchmark:** Dow Jones Global Islamic Index.
- **Target return:** Running 5 per cent tracking error on the Dow Jones Islamic Market World Index.
- **Minimum investment:** Each of the share classes has a minimum initial investment and minimum holding specified as 40,000 for share class A, 5,000,000 for share class B and 1,500 for share class C (in each of the currencies).
- **Distribution policy:** Dividends will be reinvested.
- **Management fees:** Ranging from 0.5 to 1.5 per cent per annum depending on the share class.
- **Ceilings:** Exposure to permitted assets, currencies, credit rating levels and counterparties is limited to a percentage of net asset value to ensure appropriate risk diversification.
- ***Zakat* payment:** Responsibility of the investor.

Geographical and sector exposures

The fund's investment style indicates 'portfolio of best ideas unconstrained by geography and sector', which implies that the sector and geographical weights will vary depending on the views of the fund manager on the market and its developments. As of the end of 2009, the fund holds the majority of its assets in North America and Europe (excluding the UK), with the main sectors being oil and gas, health care, technology and industrials. A variation of the fund weighting versus the weight in the index is given to provide greater clarity not only on the future expectations of the fund manager, but also to review the sector contribution to the overall return.

Performance

Providing up-to-date performance data is outside the scope of this book, and would in any case need to be verified by individual investors since it will be subject to change due to, for instance, market circumstances, changes in future expectations and developments internal to the fund. Comparing the performance for a year up to the first quarter of 2010 with those of its peers shows that the fund generally meets its benchmark of remaining within a 5 per cent tracking error on the Dow Jones Islamic Market World Index. Compared with other indices in the same peer group, such as the HSBC Amanah Global Equity Index and the MSCI World Index, the fund has, as would be expected, sometimes performed below and sometimes in excess of the indices.

Conclusion

The SWIP Islamic Global Equity Fund is actively managed and although it uses the constituents of the Dow Jones Global Islamic Index as a basis, it is not restricted to its universe and actively researches and selects additional investments for inclusion in the fund. All additional stocks in the universe are reviewed and approved by the fund's *Sharia'a* supervisory board prior to inclusion. The fund shows that exclusion of non-*Sharia'a*-compliant equity can still enable an active equity investment strategy and fulfil the requirement to build a well diversified portfolio and, although past performance is of course no guarantee for future performance, the fund has proven that it is possible to perform within a 5 per cent tracking error of its chosen benchmark index.

7.3 Fund of Funds: Al Rajhi fund range

The investment strategy of a fund of funds is not to invest in individual assets as such but in other funds and it relies heavily on the ability of the fund manager to identify outperforming funds. A fund of funds is not necessarily less volatile since the volatility in the fund will be dependent on the funds it invests in, but could offer greater diversification benefits by selecting the right mix of funds to invest in.

The example used in this case study is the fund of funds range offered by Al Rajhi Bank which consists of four different funds. The investment strategy of investing in units of selected *Sharia'a*-compliant funds is the same for each of the funds, but the actual asset allocation differs.

Background on the asset manager

Al Rajhi Capital is one of the largest fund managers in the Kingdom of Saudi Arabia and is fully *Sharia'a* compliant. Al Rajhi Capital offers a range of mutual funds which include equity, commodities, real estate and fund of funds investment solutions as well as proprietary fund management. In addition, a range of capital protected funds is offered. The funds are designed to meet the potential investment needs and risk–return profiles of a broad range of investors and invest in local, regional and global markets.

Jurisdiction of incorporation

The funds are regulated by the Capital Market Authority of Saudi Arabia, which has issued clear rules regarding investment funds, including the information that needs to be provided to investors, the minimum requirements for terms and conditions, subscription and redemption forms, marketing of the fund and other general requirements.[5] Specific regulations apply to a fund of funds which detail the following:

1. In order to be authorised as a fund of funds, the investment fund needs to invest all of its funds in other investments funds, with the exception of a proportion of assets that may be held in cash or other liquid investments.

2. The fund must be authorised and regulated under the Capital Market Authority's Investment Fund Regulations.
3. A fund of funds needs to invest in at least three investment funds, with a minimum of 5 per cent and a maximum of 50 per cent of its net asset value being invested in any one fund.
4. The terms and conditions must include the aggregate of the underlying fees of the investment fund and the fees charged by the fund of funds.

Saudi Arabia operates a relatively low tax regime, although it is more beneficial for residents than non-residents. In relation to investments, there are three different taxes that need to be considered:

1. **Taxation of investment income.** Dividends are subject to withholding tax when paid or deemed to be paid to a non-resident.
2. **Wealth taxes.** *Zakat* is levied on Saudi and GCC nationals.
3. **Capital gains tax.** The proceeds of the sale or transfer of shares in Saudi companies or partnerships is added to the income of the seller and treated as income tax.

When investing in a fund of funds, for residents and GCC nationals their investment will be included in the calculation of *zakat*, but no other taxes are due. Non-residents are subject to withholding tax on their dividends and to income tax in the event that they sell or transfer shares in Saudi companies or partnerships.

Fund objective
The objectives of the funds that are part of the Fund of Funds range is to achieve long-term capital appreciation

by investing in units of select *Sharia'a*-compliant equity and commodity funds and, in addition, aims to provide liquidity to investors. Each of the funds in the range has the same investment objectives and exclusively invests in funds offered by Al-Rajhi. The individual funds have a different investment strategy when it comes to the actual funds they invest in, and apply a different benchmark.

General fund characteristics
The funds in the Al Rajhi Fund of Funds range share a number of similar characteristics:

- **Currency:** USD.
- *Sharia'a* **supervisory board:** All funds are approved by the Al Rajhi *Sharia'a* supervisory board, with ongoing compliance being ensured by the *Sharia'a* Control Department which operates under the *Sharia'a* supervisory board. The Al Rajhi Capital *Sharia'a* supervisory board has three members.
- **Redemptions:** Bi-weekly on Tuesday and Saturday.
- **Minimum investment:** $2,000.
- **Management fees:** 2 per cent.
- **Ceilings:** Exposure to different funds that can be included are defined by law.
- *Zakat* **payment:** Responsibility of the investor.

Asset allocation and benchmark per fund
In addition to the above-mentioned generic criteria, each of the funds in the Fund of Funds range – two balanced funds, the Ladies Fund and the Children Fund – has its own asset allocations, risk profile and benchmark.

- **Al Rajhi Balanced Fund 1.** With a moderate risk level, the fund invests the vast majority of its assets (70 to 80 per cent) in commodity funds with the remaining in liquid instruments and equity funds. The fund monitors its performance against a benchmark that consists of 75 per cent of three-month $ LIBOR plus 25 per cent of the Dow Jones Islamic Market Titans Index.

- **Al Rajhi Balanced Fund 2.** Contrary to Balanced Fund 1, this fund has a moderate to high risk profile and invests a small proportion of its assets in commodity funds and liquid assets (20 to 30 per cent) with the majority (70 to 80 per cent) in equity funds. The difference in asset allocation and risk is also reflected in the fund's benchmark which consists of 40 per cent of three-month $ LIBOR plus 60 per cent of the Dow Jones Islamic Market Titans Index.

- **Al Rajhi Ladies Fund.** Like Balanced Fund 2, the Ladies Fund has a moderate to high risk level. It invests the vast majority of its assets (65 to 75 per cent) in equity funds with the remaining in liquid instruments and commodity funds. The fund's benchmark reveals a longer-term hold strategy than Balanced Fund 2, which becomes clear from the fact that the index component in the benchmark is higher. The fund monitors its performance against a benchmark that consists of 25 per cent of three-month $ LIBOR plus 75 per cent of the Dow Jones Islamic Market Titans Index.

- **Al Rajhi Children Fund.** The choice of benchmark for this fund implies an even longer investment horizon and has a moderate to high risk level. The fund invests the vast majority of its assets (80 to 90 per cent) in equity funds with the remaining in liquid instruments and commodity funds. The fund monitors its performance against a benchmark that consists of 15 per cent of three-month $ LIBOR plus 85 per cent of the Dow Jones Islamic Market Titans Index.

Geographical and sector exposures

Due to the fact that the investment mandate of the Al Rajhi fund of funds range restricts the funds to invest solely in Al Rajhi funds, the geographic and sector exposure levels are restricted to those available in the funds it can invest in. Although Al Rajhi manages a broad range of funds, the larger investment funds are those focussing on Saudi Arabia and the GCC Countries. As a result, the Fund of Funds displays an overweighting in regional investments.

There are a number of advantages to this. On the one hand, the investments are more likely to be fully *Sharia'a* compliant due to which dividend purification does not occur and all dividends are available for reinvestment. In addition, investing in local companies will directly benefit the local and regional economy. On the other hand, this also means this leads to a reduced opportunity to diversify which in turn leads to potentially higher volatility which will need to be managed in the fund.

Performance

Providing up-to-date performance data is outside the scope of this book, and would in any case need to be verified by individual investors since it will be subject to change due to, for instance, market circumstances, changes in future expectations and developments internal to the fund. The Al Rajhi Fund of Funds factsheets clearly show that since their inception in 1998 each of the funds has outperformed its benchmark in the period running up to early 2010. Particularly in later years, the funds all show significant outperformance which may point to the benchmark being set too low.

Conclusion

The Al Rajhi Fund of Funds range provides a viable, *Sharia'a*-compliant, investment alternative to a conventional fund of funds. The management fees are, at 2 per cent, relatively steep compared to similar funds in the conventional market for which the expected management fees for this type of fund would only rarely be in excess of 1 per cent. The management fee does, however, reflect the fees the fund has to pay in management fees to the funds it invests in. The performance of the funds is well in excess of its benchmark which may point to the benchmark being too low, a genuine sign of the quality of the manager, or a combination of both.

7.4 Exchange Traded Fund: i-VCAP – MyETF-DJIM25

As detailed in section 3.7, an exchange traded fund or ETF is a security that tracks an index, commodity or basket of assets in the same way as an index fund, but trades on an exchange in a way similar to that of securities. ETFs provide diversification benefits to the investor and can be bought and sold on an exchange thus providing a liquid instrument. The example used in this case study is the MyETF-DJIM25 managed by i-VCAP Management Sdn Bhd.

Background on the asset manager
i-VCAP incorporated in Malaysia on 25 October 2007 and is a wholly owned subsidiary of Valuecap Sdn Bhd, which was established in 2002 with the principal aim of investing in securities listed on Bursa Malaysia Securities Berhad.

Jurisdiction of incorporation
The MyETF-DJIM25 fund is incorporated in Malaysia and regulated by the Securities Commission of Malaysia. The fund has obtained the status 'National ETF' which is derived from the participation of seven initial fund providers which are all Malaysian corporations. The fund has been

listed on the Main Market of Bursa Securities since 31 January 2008.

Fund objective
The fund's objective is to invest in *Sharia'a*-compliant assets providing investment results that closely correspond to the performance of the benchmark index, regardless of its performance. It is not aiming to outperform the index, but instead aims to track it with the lowest possible tracking error.

General fund characteristics
The MyETF-DJIM25 index provides a liquid, low-cost financial instrument for investors seeking a performance generally similar to the benchmark index. Although designed to be a liquid instrument, the fund units can equally have a place as a medium- to long-term investment in a diversified portfolio.

The fund tracks the Dow Jones Islamic Market Malaysia Titans 25 Index, which is a market capitalisation weighted, free-float adjusted index provided by Dow Jones created on 18 January 2008. It contains 25 *Sharia'a*-compliant securities listed on the Bursa Malaysia. The securities are selected applying the Dow Jones screening process, described in detail in Chapter 3. The constituents of the index are weighted by market capitalisation. Under certain predefined circumstances, the fund manager is entitled to change the benchmark index.

The general characteristics of the fund can be summarised as follows:

- **Currency:** Malaysian ringgit.
- *Sharia'a* **supervisory board:** CIMB Islamic.
- **Benchmark:** Dow Jones Islamic Market Malaysia Titans 25.

- **Target return:** Dow Jones Islamic Market Malaysia Titans 25.
- **Management fees:** 0.4 per cent plus an annual trustee fee of 0.05 per cent and an index licence fee of 0.04 per cent.
- **Distribution policy:** Semi-annual.
- **Eligible investors:** Institutional investors and Malaysian retail investors over the age of 18.
- *Zakat* **payment:** Responsibility of the investor.

Generic asset allocation

The asset allocation for the MyETF-DJIM25 index is fairly straightforward, with a maximum of 10 per cent that can be invested in liquid assets.

The fund manager can invest in any of the following assets:

- equity of the index constituents;
- equity of previous constituents of the index provided that they will be disposed of within a reasonable period;
- equity not part of the index to a maximum of 5 per cent provided that it has a high correlation to the index

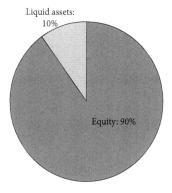

Figure 7.3 *MyETF-DJM25 asset allocation*

constituent and only in the event of liquidity constraints with the constituents;

- *Sharia'a*-compliant collective investment schemes to a maximum of 10 per cent of the fund's assets; and
- any other approved investment.

Geographical exposure

Due to the fact that the fund is tracking the Dow Jones Islamic Market Malaysia Titans 25, the fund is fully exposed to the Malaysian economy. As a result, investors already having a large concentration of Malaysian risk may find the MyETF-DJIM25 fund a less attractive alternative. However, there are a number of advantages. For example, the constituents of the index are more likely to be fully *Sharia'a* compliant which means no purification of income would be required. In addition, investing in Malaysian-based companies stimulates the local economy.

Performance

Providing up-to-date performance data is outside the scope of this book, and would in any case need to be verified by individual investors since it will be subject to change due to, for instance, market circumstances and developments internal to the fund. Since inception, the fund has managed to stay within its limit of a 3 per cent tracking error and has been performing slightly above the index.

Conclusion

The MyETF-DJIM25 fund has, although relatively new, performed in line with its benchmark and shows that Islamic ETFs are a viable alternative to non-*Sharia'a*-compliant ETFs. The performance is in line with the benchmark whilst charging management fees that are roughly in line with those that would be charged for a comparable conventional

ETF. The fund has performed well during its first year of incorporation and the future outlook is positive.

7.5 Concluding remarks

The case studies included in this chapter show that there is a wide range of *Sharia'a*-compliant funds in the market, and those displayed here simply provide an example of the potential investment opportunities available to *Sharia'a*-compliant investors. The range of fund types such as fixed income funds, ETFs and index funds match the fund types available to conventional investors and the universe is ever expanding. In addition, the funds cover a wide range of geographies and sectors. The examples show that the funds are capable of performing in line with their benchmarks, although in some cases the management fees are still on the high side. At this point in time, many funds have lowered their management fees to levels more in line with conventional funds and as the market develops, it is expected that this trend will continue.

Notes
1. Law of 13 February 2007 relating to specialised investment funds.
2. BLME $ Income Fund factsheet, dated 31 March 2010.
3. BLME $ Income Fund factsheet, dated 31 March 2010.
4. Source: SWIP.
5. Capital Market Authority – Investment Funds Regulations. Based on the Capital Market Law, issued by Royal Decree No. M/30, December 2006.

CHAPTER 8
SUMMARY AND CONCLUDING REMARKS

The number and variety of *Sharia'a*-compliant investment funds available in the market has increased significantly over the past number of years and is expected to continue to grow at a pace similar to that of the overall Islamic financial industry. So far, many funds have only attracted relatively low levels of investment with the majority of the funds being well below $100 million assets under management. As the market matures, this is set to change, and new funds that are introduced show that there is certainly a desire to achieve larger fund sizes.

The ethical principles underpinning Islamic ethics are defined within *Sharia'a*, which governs every aspect of a Muslim's life and dealings with others including commerce. The Islamic financial system works on the basis of these principles and values, many of which are universally applicable and are often not dissimilar to the norms and values associated with strong business ethics often advocated by professional industry bodies and the generally accepted view of social responsibility. One of the overarching principles in *Sharia'a* is justice, which defines how different parties should be dealing with each other in business as well as in a larger social context and includes guidance regarding the principles of fairness and justice between parties in a contract. The principles of Islamic ethics include integrity, stewardship, sincerity, justness in exchange and charitable giving.

The principles of Islamic ethics in turn translate into a set of behavioural norms and values applicable to business which include honesty, fair trade, disclosure, transparency and avoidance of misrepresentation as well as prohibitions on certain assets and industries, hoarding, speculation, gambling and interest. The prohibitions in particular have an impact on *Sharia'a*-compliant fund management since they restrict the types of instrument as well as the industries that can be invested in. Prohibited industries cover conventional financial services, alcohol, pork, gambling, tobacco, adult entertainment and weaponry.

Islamic asset management, like any other part of the Islamic financial industry, needs to work within the ethical framework identified by *Sharia'a*, and its operations, the fund mandate and its investments need to be compliant with the principles of *Sharia'a*. At the same time, Islamic asset management fulfils a role similar to that of conventional asset management and provides the opportunity to invest in a diversified pool of assets, providing access to the benefits of large scale against relatively small invested amounts with the expectation of a monetary gain.

Sharia'a-compliant funds generally accept investors' funds under one of two different structures: *mudaraba* or *wakala*. In both structures the investor take the risk of losing their capital. As a direct result of the requirement for *Sharia'a* compliance, the fund manager is restricted to a smaller investment universe and is hampered by the limited availability of a risk free asset.

The financial instruments available to the *Sharia'a*-compliant fund manager as well as the assets they can invest in need to comply with all prohibitions including those on short selling. Although in some ways this limits the investment universe, there still is a range of instrument types that can be applied, such as:

- direct investments and venture capital applying *mudaraba* and *musharaka* transactions
- public and private equity
- interbank deposits and short-term placements using *wakala*, commodity *murabaha*, *tawarruq* and *salam* transactions
- leasing (*ijara*)
- project finance using *salam* and *istisna* transactions
- foreign exchange
- unilateral promises (*wa'd*)
- down payment (*arbun*)
- bond type instruments (*sukuk*).

These instruments are applied in a wide range of funds which covers the full spectrum from low risk and low return to high risk and potentially high returns or large possible losses. Within the *Sharia'a*-compliant fund universe, the structures observed are typically similar to conventional structures available in the market with only few differences. The *Sharia'a*-compliant fund structure is generally a mutual fund structure and encompasses a board of directors, fund managers, analysts, administrators, custodians and all other functions typically applicable. In addition to all the usual functions, a *Sharia'a*-compliant fund also has a *Sharia'a* supervisory board which is typically made up of three to five members who are appointed prior to the incorporation of the fund and are responsible for ensuring that the fund is and remains compliant. Ultimate responsibility for *Sharia'a* compliance, however, lies with the board of directors of the fund. It is important to note that the *Sharia'a* supervisory board is not responsible for any operational, strategic or investment decisions the fund manager makes as long as the fund continues to be *Sharia'a* compliant.

The *Sharia'a*-compliant fund universe contains a wide range of fund types including:

- **Fixed income.** Also known as money market funds, fixed income funds can roughly be divided into five different categories based on the risk–return characteristics and generally invest in a combination of instruments to generate a return on liquid assets. The majority of outperformance of a fixed income fund is typically generated by instruments with longer maturities with the necessary liquidity provided by short-term instruments. The actual asset allocation of a fixed income fund depends on where the fund is positioned on the risk–return curve. As a broad rule of thumb, the fixed income funds can be divided in five main types: deposit funds; liquidity funds; money market funds; enhanced cash funds; and high yield funds.
- **Lease fund.** Generally considered slightly higher risk with a potential to provide a higher return, lease funds generally invest in a diversified pool of leases combined with short-term placements to provide liquidity to the fund.
- **Commodity fund.** A commodity fund invests in a diversified range of commodities. With the price of commodities being more volatile over time, the fund is aiming for a higher return, but also has the potential for larger losses.
- **Real estate fund.** A real estate fund invests in commercial and residential real estate to generate a yield from rental income and appreciation of the property values.
- **Equity fund.** Equity funds invest in public or pri-

vate equity or index trackers. The underlying equity is selected based on industry and financial screens which ensure the investment is *Sharia'a* compliant.

- **Exchange traded fund (ETF).** ETFs track an index, commodity or basket of assets, like an index fund, but trade on an exchange like a stock.

- **Hedge fund.** A hedge fund invests in a variety of instruments for risk diversification by applying short selling and derivatives. Short selling and speculation are prohibited in *Sharia'a* which rules out the implementation of hedge funds in a *Sharia'a*-compliant manner. However, hedging excessive risk is deemed to be prudent. *Sharia'a*-compliant hedge funds have so far not really materialised.

Initially, *Sharia'a*-compliant funds were benchmarked against conventional indices to indicate their performance relative to the market. More recently, the major conventional index providers have developed their own range of *Sharia'a*-compliant indices which provide an appropriate alternative for *Sharia'a*-compliant funds. Each of the index series applies industry and financial ratios which differ slightly, but not significantly, from the screening criteria outlined in AAOIFI *Sharia'a* standard 21. Even the most thorough screening process, however, cannot prevent a company or real estate asset that a fund has invested in from potentially becoming non-compliant, for example due to a change in strategy, change of use or a merger. In the event this situation is temporary, the asset is generally allowed to remain in the investment universe but will be monitored closely. If the asset is not expected to come back to compliance, disinvestment is required. Typically disinvestment will be allowed to take place over a period of time in order to protect investor interests.

Often incorporated and authorised in Western jurisdictions, *Sharia'a*-compliant funds have to follow the same rules and regulations regarding processing, reporting and compliance as conventional funds. In addition, *Sharia'a*-compliant funds will have to ensure all their transactions and operations are in line with the requirements of *Sharia'a*.

The processes for redemptions, switches, subscriptions, payments and receipts are all similar to the processes in place for a conventional fund. Periodically, the administrator determines the value of the assets held in each of the different funds and fund compartments under its responsibility. The exact calculation of the value of an asset is dependent on the asset and the valuation methodology defined in the fund strategy and can be based on fair value, straight line or historic cost.

In addition to the risks inherent with fund management such as liquidity risk, credit risk and counterparty risk, *Sharia'a*-compliant funds also run risks associated with Islamic financial institutions such as fiduciary risk, displaced commercial risk and rate of return risk which need to be managed within the confines of the fund and investment strategy.

Each *Sharia'a*-compliant fund has its own *Sharia'a* supervisory board which is appointed prior to the incorporation of the fund with the responsibility for initial and ongoing *Sharia'a* compliance. Ultimate responsibility for *Sharia'a* compliance lies with the board of directors and non-compliance could result in negligence, which can have severe repercussions. Opining on the suitability of an investment beyond its *Sharia'a* compliance is however outside of the scope of the *Sharia'a* supervisory board's remit.

Generally, *Sharia'a*-compliant funds have similar characteristics to those of conventional funds and offer diversified investment strategies to *Sharia'a*-compliant investors. The main differences between *Sharia'a*-compliant and conventional funds are associated with the types of instrument that can be applied, the industries that can be invested in and the fact that they have an additional level of governance represented by the *Sharia'a* supervisory board.

The Islamic asset management industry is growing in line with the growth of the overall Islamic finance industry, and the variety of funds available is expanding. Although the average size of assets under management is still relatively low, as track records are becoming available and investor confidence is building, the interest in *Sharia'a*-compliant asset management is likely to increase.

The examples included in this book support this view and although only a small, randomly chosen number of funds is included, they clearly show that there is a wide range of *Sharia'a*-compliant funds available to investors. The range of fund types such as fixed income funds, ETFs and index funds match the fund types available to conventional investors that cover a wide range of geographies and sectors.

Arabic is a phonetic language and all words are spelled exactly as they sound. Because the Arabic alphabet differs from the English, and English is less phonetic in nature, different English translations are available for the common words in Islamic finance. This glossary contains abbreviations used in the text as well as definitions of all Arabic terms used.

aʿqd	contract or transaction executed between two or more parties for mutual benefit
AAOIFI	Accounting and Auditing Organization for Islamic Financial Institutions
arbun	down payment on a sales contract in which the buyer has not paid the full price or taken possession of the good. The deposit is non-refundable. The buyer can opt to cancel the contract
CDO	collateralised debt obligation
CDS	credit default swap
CIO	chief investment officer
CIS	capital investment scheme
CSSF	Commission de Surveillance du Secteur Financier
DJIM	Dow Jones Islamic Markets Indexes
EEA	European Economic Area
ETF	exchange traded fund
EVCA	European Private Equity and Venture Capital Association

fatwa	declaration in Islam provided by an Islamic legal specialist
fiqh	understanding of the (Islamic) law
fiqh al muamalat	Islamic commercial jurisprudence
FSA	Financial Services Authority
GCC	Gulf Cooperation Council. Economic cooperation between Bahrain, Kuwait, Oman, Qatar, Saudi Arabia and the United Arab Emirates
gharar	to deceive, cheat, delude, lure, entice and overall uncertainty. Also defined as '*gharar* is whose consequences are hidden' or 'the sale of probable items whose existence or characteristics are not certain'
hadith	a narrative record of the sayings and actions of the Prophet
halal	permitted
haram	prohibited
hawala	the transfer of money from one person to another. The recipient may charge administration charges which should not be proportionate to the sum of money
ICB	industry classification benchmark
ijara	a bilateral contract allowing the sale of the usufruct for a specified rent and a specified period. A lease
ijara muntahia bittamleek	lease ending in ownership. A finance lease structure in which the lessee has the option to exercise their right to purchase the asset at any time during the lease period
ijara wa iqtina	a lease with transfer of ownership at the end of the lease period or finance lease. Variations exist such as the *ijara muntahia*

	bittamleek which is a finance lease structure in which the lessee has the option to exercise their right to purchase the asset at any time during the lease period
ijtihad	interpretation of the Quran and *Sunnah* by independent jurists
istisna	sale with deferred delivery. Payment can be in a lump sum in advance or progressively in accordance with progress made. Delivery of goods is deferred
IT	investment trust
kafala	guarantee or third-party obligation
KYC	know your customer
LIBOR	London Interbank Offer Rate
maysir	gambling; games of chance
MiFID	Markets in Financial Investments Directive
muamalat	activities not explicitly governed by *Sharia'a* with respect to worship
mudaraba	partnership contract; sub-set of *musharaka*
mudarib	party in a contract providing knowledge and skill
murabaha	deferred payment sale or instalment credit sale
musharaka	partnership contract
NAV	net asset value
OECD	Organisation for Economic Co-operation and Development
OEIC	open-ended investment company
OTC	over the counter
parallel salam	a parallel contract to an existing *salam* contract to hedge the *salam* position. Often an outright sale (with deferred delivery), but could be arranged with payment at a later

	date using an LC or guarantee to secure the payment
qard	loan
qard al hassan	an interest free loan, often used in a charitable context. The recipient has the moral obligation to repay the principal
Quran	Book of God
rab al mal	party in a contract providing finances
rahn	collateral pledged
re-takaful	Islamic re-insurance undertaken to reduce excessive concentration risks
riba	interest
riba al fadl	excess compensation without any consideration (e.g. monies passing between the parties) resulting from an exchange of sale of goods
riba al naseeyah	excess resulting from predetermined interest which a lender receives over and above the principal amount it has lent out. Primary form of *riba*. It is the addition of a premium paid to the lender in return for waiting for their money. (Time value of money)
S&P	Standard & Poor's
sadaqat	voluntary charitable contribution, guided by the goodwill of the donor
sakk	see *sukuk*, below
salam	sale with deferred delivery. Payment is paid in full and up front, delivery of good is deferred
sarf	purchase and sale of currency. Only allowed at spot for equal value
Sharia'a	ethical framework of Islam, often referred to as Islamic law

SICAV	*société d'investissement à capital variable*
SPV	special purpose vehicle
SSB	*Sharia'a* supervisory board
sukuk	plural of *sakk*. Represents partial ownership in assets. *Sukuk* are technically neither shares nor bonds but have characteristics of both. Profit is based on the performance of the underlying assets or projects
Sunnah	words or acts of the prophet
tabarru'	non-commercial donation or gift. Any benefit that is given by a person to another without getting anything in exchange
takaful	Islamic insurance comparable to mutual insurance
tawarruq	purchase of a commodity that is immediately sold on to a third party (usually using the original seller as agent) on spot for cash. Form of reverse *murabaha*
UCITS	undertakings for collective investments in transferable securities
UT	unit trust
VAR	value at risk
VAT	value added tax
wa'd	unilateral promise. An undertaking or promise by one party to do or not do something in the future
wakala	agency contract. Often applied to brokerage, asset management and investment activities
wakil	agent in a *wakala* or agency contract
zakat	obligatory donation to charity for those who can afford it

BIBLIOGRAPHY

AAOIFI (2002), *Accounting, Auditing and Governance Standards for Islamic Financial Institutions*, Bahrain: AAOIFI.

AAOIFI (2008), *Sharia'a Standards for Islamic Financial Institutions*, Bahrain: AAOIFI.

Ahmed, O. B. (2001), *Islamic Equity Funds: The Mode of Resource Mobilisation and Placement*, Jeddah: Islamic Research and Training Institute.

Al-Deehani, T., R. A. A. Karim and V. Murinde (1999), 'The Capital Structure of Islamic Banks under the Contractual Obligation of Profit Sharing', *International Journal of Theoretical and Applied Finance*, 2(3), pp. 243–83.

Ali, Rahail (ed.) (2008), *Islamic Finance: A Practical Guide*, London: Globe Law and Business.

Archer, S., and R. A. A. Karim (2001), *On Capital Structure, Risk Sharing and Capital Adequacy in Islamic Banks*, ABACUS, under review.

Archer, S., and R. A. A. Karim (2006), 'On Capital Structure, Risk Sharing and Capital Adequacy in Islamic Banks', *International Journal of Theoretical and Applied Finance*, 9(3), pp. 269–80.

Bernstein, Peter L. (1998), *Against the Gods: The Remarkable Story of Risk*, New York: John Wiley & Sons.

Bolt, W. and A. F. Tieman (2004), *Banking Competition, Risk, and Regulation*, IMF Working Paper WP/04/11, Washington, DC: IMF.

Bookstaber, R. (1999), 'Risk Management in Complex Organizations', *Financial Analysts Journal*, 54(2), pp. 18–20.

Boyd, J. H. and M. Gertler (1994), 'Are Banks Dead? Or, Are the Reports Greatly Exaggerated?', in *Conference Proceedings, The (Declining?) Role of Banking*, 30th Annual Conference on Bank Structure and Competition, Chicago: Federal Reserve Bank of Chicago, pp. 85–117.

Brealey, R. A., S. C. Myers and A. J. Marcus (2003), *Fundamentals of Corporate Finance*, international edition, New York: McGraw-Hill.

Chartered Institute for Securities and Investment (2009), *Islamic Finance Qualification*, edition 3, London: CISI.

Çizakça, M. (1996), *A Comparative Evolution of Business Partnerships – The Islamic World and Europe, With Specific Reference to the Ottoman Archives*, Leiden: E. J. Brill.

DeLorenzo, Y. T. (undated), *The Total Returns Swap and the 'Shariah Conversion Technology' Stratagem*, http://www.failaka.com/downloads/DeLorenzo_TotalReturnsSwap.pdf, accessed 24 March 2010.

Ferri, R. A, (2009), *The ETF Book: All You Need to Know About Exchange-Traded Funds*, Hoboken: John Wiley & Sons Inc.

Jaffr, S. (ed.) (2004), *Islamic Asset Management: Forming the Future for Shari'a-Compliant Investment Strategies*, London: Euromoney Books.

Markowitz, H. (1952), 'Portfolio Selection', *The Journal of Finance*, 12(1), pp. 77–91.

Marshall, A. (1895), *Principles of Economics*, 3rd edition, London: Macmillan & Co.

Merton, R. C. and A. F. Perold (1993), 'Theory of Risk Capital in Financial Firms', *Journal of Applied Corporate Finance*, 6(3), pp. 16–33.

Nienhaus, V. (2001), 'Transparency, Governance and Risk Management in Islamic Financial Institutions: Roles of Stakeholders in Islamic Financial Institutions', paper presented to the conference Transparency, Governance and Risk Management in Islamic Financial Institutions, Beirut.

OECD (2004), *Policy Brief: The OECD Principles of Corporate Governance*, Paris: OECD Observer.

OECD (2004a), *OECD Principles of Corporate Governance*, Paris: OECD.

Oxford Dictionary of Finance and Banking (1997), 2nd edition, Oxford: Oxford University Press.

Roache, S. K. and M. Rossi (2009), *The Effects of Economic News on Commodity Prices: Is Gold Just Another Commodity?*, IMF working paper 09/140, Washington, DC: IMF.

Rosly, S. A. and M. A. A Bakar (2003), 'Performance of Islamic and Mainstream Banks in Malaysia', *International Journal of Social Economics*, 30(12), pp. 1249–65.

Schoon, N. (2008), *Islamic Banking and Finance*, London: Spiramus Press.

Sharpe, W. F. (1964), 'Capital Asset Prices: A Theory of Market Equilibrium under Conditions of Risk', *The Journal of Finance*, 19(3), pp. 425–42.

Smith, A. (1795), *The Theory of Moral Sentiments*, London: A. Millar.

Smith, A. (1881), *An Inquiry into the Nature and Causes of the Wealth of Nations*, abridged version with notes and appendices by Wolsely P. Emerton, MA BCL, Oxford: James Thornton.

Standard & Poor's (2002), *Classic Ratings Approach Applied to Islamic Banks despite Industry Specifics*, London: 27 November 2002.

Sundararajan, V. and L. Errico (2002), *Islamic Financial*

Institutions and Products in the Global Financial System: Key Issues in Risk Management and Challenges Ahead, IMF working paper WP/02/192, Washington, DC: IMF.

Tomkins, C. and R. A. A. Karim (1987), 'The *Shari'ah* and its Implications for Islamic Financial Analysis: An Opportunity to Study Interactions Among Society, Organisation, and Accounting, *The American Journal of Islamic Social Sciences,* 4(1), pp. 101–15.

Tran, V. Q. (2006), *Evaluating Hedge Fund Performance,* Hoboken: John Wiley & Sons Inc.

Vogel, F. E. and Hayes III, S. L. (1998), *Islamic Law and Finance – Religion, Risk, and Return,* Den Haag: Kluwer Law International.

INDEX

Note: n refers to an endnote, f to a figure, t to a table.

EU Authorised Representative: Easy Access System Europe Mustamäe tee 5
0, 10621 Tallinn, Estonia gpsr.requests@easproject.com

Printed and bound by CPI Group (UK) Ltd, Croydon, CR0 4YY
16/04/2025
01846984-0001